Ad Limina ADDRESSES

THE ADDRESSES OF
HIS HOLINESS
POPE JOHN PAUL II
TO THE BISHOPS OF THE
UNITED STATES

FEBRUARY 1998-OCTOBER 1998

INCLUDES
THE BISHOPS' GREETINGS

During 1998, the U.S. bishops traveled to Rome in thirteen regional groupings for their *Ad Limina* visits, which they are required to make every five years. While in Rome each group of bishops concelebrated Mass with the Holy Father, Pope John Paul II, in his private chapel after which the Holy Father addressed the bishops. The texts of the Holy Father's addresses to the U.S. bishops and the greetings offered by a member of each region on behalf of the bishops of the respective regions have been compiled by the General Secretariat and are reproduced herein. This compilation has been reviewed by Most Rev. Anthony M. Pilla, president of the National Conference of Catholic Bishops, and is authorized for publication by the undersigned.

Monsignor Dennis M. Schnurr
General Secretary, NCCB/USCC

SCRIPTURE TEXTS USED IN THIS WORK ARE TAKEN FROM THE FOLLOWING:

The Catholic Edition of the Revised Standard Version of the Bible, copyright © 1965, 1966 by the Division of Christian Education of the National Council of the Churches of Christ in the United States of America. Used by permission. All rights reserved. (abbreviated as RSV in the text)

New American Bible, copyright © 1970 by the Confraternity of Christian Doctrine, Washington, D.C. 20017. Used by permission of copyright owner. All rights reserved. (abbreviated as NAB 1970 in the text)

New American Bible, copyright © 1991, 1986, and 1970 by the Confraternity of Christian Doctrine, Washington, D.C. 20017. Used by permission of copyright owner. All rights reserved. (abbreviated as NAB in the text)

The New Jerusalem Bible, copyright © 1985, Darton, Longman & Todd, Ltd. and Doubleday & Company, Inc. Used by permission. All rights reserved. (abbreviated as NJB in the text)

New Revised Standard Version Bible: Catholic Edition, copyright © 1989, 1993, Division of Christian Education of the National Council of the Churches of Christ in the United States of America. Used by permission. All rights reserved. (abbreviated as NRSV in the text)

Excerpts from *The Documents of Vatican II,* Walter M. Abbott, SJ, General Editor, copyright © 1966 by America Press, Inc. Reprinted with permission. All rights reserved.

Region II Bishops' Greeting from *L'Osservatore Romano*. Used by permission. All rights reserved.

First Printing, November 1998

ISBN 1-57455-288-0

Copyright © 1998, United States Catholic Conference, Inc., Washington, D.C. All rights reserved. No part of this work may be reproduced or transmitted in any form or by any means, electronic or mechanical, including photocopying, recording, or by any information storage and retrieval system, without permission in writing from the copyright holder.

262.12
Cat

CONTENTS

PREFACE

During 1998, the U.S. bishops made their *Ad Limina* visits to the Holy See. Diocesan bishops make a report about their dioceses to the Holy Father every five years. They present these reports during visits to Rome. If a diocese has a coadjutor or auxiliary bishops, they too usually make these visits. The full title *Ad Limina Apostolorum* means literally "to the thresholds of the apostles" and comes from the custom of praying at the tombs of the apostles Peter and Paul, who were martyred in Rome.

During these visits, the bishops submit their reports and call on the departments (or "dicasteries") of the Holy See with which they may have special business. One highlight is the personal meeting each diocesan bishop has with the Holy Father. It is a unique opportunity to sense his shepherd's care of Christ's entire flock in both its unity and its diversity.

Another highlight is commemorated in this book, and it is the address the Holy Father gives to each group of bishops from a particular nation. The visits of the U.S. bishops are arranged according to the thirteen regions into which the provinces and dioceses of the United States have been grouped to facilitate communication and the activities of the National Conference of Catholic Bishops/United States Catholic Conference.

In this volume, you will find these thirteen talks that Pope John Paul II gave beginning in February 1998 and concluding the following October listed in chronological order. In his first talk, the Holy Father laid down the overall plan for his presentations. He told this region of bishops that the coming grace and blessings of the millennium jubilee had been "prepared by that extraordinary ecclesial event of recent times, the Second Vatican Council." Therefore, his talks to the U.S. bishops throughout the year would "reflect on certain themes of the council, in an effort to discern how best we can ensure that all that God wishes for the Church will become a reality."

This plan provided a firm foundation on which the Holy Father erected the complex and beautiful structure that are his 1998 *Ad Limina* addresses. Under its roof are contained a rich variety of insights, instruction, admonition, and inspiration, which all readers will find as valuable and spiritually enriching as did the bishops themselves. Also included are the remarks offered by the senior prelate of each region to the Holy Father before his address.

It is appropriate to make these talks conveniently available in one volume not only to commemorate these visits but also and especially to celebrate the blessings that God has given the Church throughout this pontificate, as Pope John Paul II celebrates the twentieth anniversary of his election as Peter's successor and as Christ's vicar. This is the fourth set of *Ad Limina* visits that the bishops of the United States have made since that election. Extraordinary as this fact may be as a statistic, it is even more extraordinary as an experience of a Holy Father who has had the opportunity to come to know us well and who has invited us to know him as a brother.

Towards the end of the Gospel of St. John, there is the moving scene where the Lord asks Peter, "Do you love me?" To Peter's positive response, the Lord says, "Feed my sheep." The bishops of the United States and of the whole world have come to know Pope John Paul II as one who can say with the sincerity of Peter himself, "Lord, you know everything. You know well that I love you." Because of that love he can feed us, his brothers and his flock, abundantly, as this volume proves.

MOST REV. WILLIAM S. SKYLSTAD
BISHOP OF SPOKANE
CHAIRMAN, AD HOC COMMITTEE
ON BISHOPS' LIFE AND MINISTRY

GREETING
OF THE BISHOPS
Region II

Your Holiness:

A s we gather here, we are poignantly reminded: "*Ubi Petrus, ibi Ecclesia.*" Your Holiness, the bishops of the New York Province truly believe that when we are with the Holy Father we are with Peter. One might compare this *Ad Limina* visit to that of the renewal of marriage vows—every five years we repeat our loyalty, commitment, and most importantly, our love for each other. I can say with confidence that every bishop of the New York Province is loyal and committed and, most importantly, loves the Church and the Holy Father.

The province of bishops and I are grateful to the various dicasteries which we have visited as a region during this week and will visit today. We have been honest with them in our discussions and they, in turn, have been honest with us and very kind to us. I can honestly say that the dicasteries want to support us and we have spoken in an effort to promote the working relationship among us.

Also, every bishop of this province accepts fully and entirely the teaching of the Church and the magisterium. To such we pledge our fidelity and loyalty, especially to the Holy Father. In our ministry, above all, we seek to be pastors of souls first and administrators, theologians, and canonists second. We know that the letter of the law can kill and the Spirit can give life, and we understand the delicate balance between the two. At the same time, we respect the law and know that it must be obeyed. At times we are misrepresented, at times we make mistakes out of human weakness rather than malice. We look to the Holy Father as our model in striking the essential balance required.

We try our best to feed the people of God with the truths of the faith. We do not deny our mistakes but we make every effort to manifest our love and concern for them at all times, and we accept correction when we have erred. We want to be obedient, and regret any failures along these lines.

Once again, Your Holiness, we express our gratitude along with the pledge of our abiding prayers and support, and above all, our love.

CARDINAL JOHN O'CONNOR
ARCHBISHOP OF NEW YORK

ADDRESS OF POPE JOHN PAUL II

Region II

Dear Brother Bishops:

1. Beginning this series of *Ad Limina* visits of the pastors of the Church in the United States, I cordially welcome you, the first group of bishops—from the ecclesiastical region of New York—and I send warm greetings to all the members of the bishops' conference. In meeting you, my first thought is to give heartfelt praise to God for the Catholic community in your country as you seek to be ever more subject to the Lord in love and fidelity (cf. Eph 5:24), pressing forward amid the trials of this world and the consolations of God, announcing the saving cross and death of the Lord until he comes (cf. 1 Cor 11:26).

In particular I express my thanks to you and your brother bishops for the spiritual friendship and the communion in faith and love which unite us in the service of the Gospel. I thank you for all the ways in which you share my pastoral concern for the universal Church. All through the years of my pontificate I have had countless opportunities to experience the characteristic love and solidarity of the Catholics of the United States for the successor of St. Peter. In this year of preparation for the Great Jubilee, dedicated to the Holy Spirit, I pray that "the Lord, the giver of life" will reward the Church in the United States with his strengthening and consoling gifts.

2. The jubilee calls us to remember and celebrate the blessings that the Father has showered upon us in Jesus Christ, the Lord of history and

the "chief shepherd" of our souls (cf. 1 Pt 5:4). Freed from sin and washed in the blood of the Lamb, we have truly become children of God, able to turn to him in absolute confidence. For we know that he loves us and will never abandon us.

Although our ministry constantly reminds us of the sufferings of so many of our fellow human beings, especially the poor and those who are persecuted for their faith in Christ, we are confident that, as the third millennium approaches, God is preparing a great springtime for Christianity (cf. *Redemptoris Missio*, no. 86).

Through the incarnation of the Son of God, eternity has entered into time. Time itself has become the dramatic arena in which the history of salvation unfolds; thus anniversaries and jubilees become times of grace—"a day blessed by the Lord," "a year of the Lord" (cf. *Tertio Millennio Adveniente*, no. 32). The Great Jubilee of the Year 2000 will be a time of unique blessings for the Church and for the world, a grace already prepared by that extraordinary ecclesial event of recent times, the Second Vatican Council, the fruits of which are still maturing toward their fullness. Since the documents of the council represent the fundamental point of reference for the Church's understanding of herself and her mission in this period of history, it is fitting that our preparation for the jubilee should involve a serious meditation on how we as bishops have received and implemented the rich body of teaching elaborated by the council fathers (cf. *Tertio Millennio Adveniente*, no. 36). In my meetings this year with the bishops of the United States, I propose to reflect on certain themes of the council in an effort to discern how best we can ensure that all that God wishes for the Church will become a reality.

3. What is the greatest challenge before us as bishops of the Church? What is the greatest need of our contemporaries? The men and women of today, like those of every time and place, are yearning for salvation. They wish to rediscover the truth of God's dominion over cre-

ation and history, to encounter his self-revelation and to experience his merciful love in all the dimensions of their lives. The great truth to be proclaimed to this and every age is that God has entered human history so that men and women can truly become children of God. The *Dogmatic Constitution on Divine Revelation (Dei Verbum)* clearly reminds us that the truth we proclaim is no human wisdom, but depends completely on God's revelation of himself. "God chose to reveal Himself and to make known to us the hidden purpose of His will (cf. Eph 1:9) by which through Christ, the Word made flesh, man has access to the Father in the Holy Spirit and comes to share in the divine nature" *(Dei Verbum*, no. 2). This is the heart of the Christian message and the essential truth which bishops must preach "in season and out of season" (2 Tm 4:2 [RSV]).

In the apostolic letter *Tertio Millennio Adveniente,* I posed the question, "To what extent has the word of God become more fully the soul of theology and the inspiration of the whole of Christian living, as *Dei Verbum* sought?" (no. 36). From everyone, but especially from the bishops, fidelity to the revealed word requires an attitude of attentive, prayerful receptivity. It requires that we allow ourselves to be renewed and transformed by our encounter with his living word. Then we will be able to help the faithful to understand that holy Scripture is a gift which we receive within the Church. It is not merely a "text" to be analyzed; it is above all an invitation to communion with the Lord. It must be read and received in a spirit of openness to that invitation.

This does not imply an uncritical approach to Scripture, but it does warn against readings informed by a sterile rationalism or by cultural pressures that compromise biblical truth. These approaches close the ear to God's call and empty the sacred text of its power to save (cf. Rom 1:16). St. Paul gives thanks to God for those who have accepted Scripture for what it really is: the word of God at work in the community of believers (cf. 1 Thes 4:13).

Tribute must be paid to the many excellent Catholic exegetes and theologians in the United States who have been untiring in their efforts to help the Christian people to understand more clearly the word of God in Scripture "so that they can better accept [it] in order to live in full communion with God" (Address on the Interpretation of the Bible in the Church, no. 9, April 23, 1993). This important work will bear the fruit the council intended if it is sustained by a vigorous spiritual life within the believing community. Only the love that issues "from a pure heart, a good conscience, and sincere faith" (1 Tm 1:5 [NAB]) enables us to understand the language of God who is love (cf. 1 Jn 4:8).

4. If the new evangelization is to be effective, our catechesis must convey the full truth of the Gospel, for that fullness of truth is the very source of our capacity to teach with authority: an authority which the faithful easily recognize when we address the essentials and deliver what we have received (cf. 1 Cor 15:3). Our "teaching office is not above the word of God, but serves it, teaching only what has been handed on, listening to it devoutly [*pie audit*], guarding it scrupulously [*sancte custodit*], and explaining it faithfully [*fideliter exponit*] by divine commission and with the help of the Holy Spirit" (*Dei Verbum*, no. 10).

Through the ministry of preaching and teaching, the whole believing community must come to see and to love Scripture and Tradition, which together lead us to understand God's salvific presence in history and show the path to real communion of life with him. In this way the entire Church will enter more deeply into the mystery of salvation and will come to appreciate that human history is the place of encounter between God and man, the place in which communion with God is offered, received, and built up.

5. The gospel message remains ever the same, yet we proclaim it in a culture which is undergoing constant transformation. We need to

reflect on the dynamics of contemporary culture in order to discern the signs of the times which affect the proclamation of the saving message of Christ. On the one hand, everywhere we see people's desire for freedom and happiness, and this speaks to us of a deep spiritual hunger. People seek to satisfy this hunger in many ways; but the failure of many proposed solutions, be they philosophies, ideologies, or fashions, has led to a great unease, if not a current of despair, in contemporary culture. Ours is often called a time of uncertainty; this uncertainty, raised to a principle by which it is denied that we can ever know the truth of things, affects the moral life, the life of prayer, and the theological correctness of people's faith (cf. *Tertio Millennio Adveniente*, no. 36).

On the other hand, many people are increasingly aware that in order to build free, just, and prosperous societies, and so create the conditions for satisfying the deepest and noblest aspirations of the human spirit, the culture through which they interact and communicate must correspond to certain basic truths about the human person.

My last visit to your country took place in 1995, during the fiftieth anniversary celebration of the United Nations. At the General Assembly I expressed the conviction that an acceleration of the human quest for freedom is one of the great dynamics of modern history in every part of the world. That dynamic shows itself clearly in the claims of the world's peoples for a fuller share in determining the political and economic choices which affect them (cf. Address to the 50th General Assembly of the United Nations, no. 2, October 5, 1995). In the unfolding of history do we not see the gradual advance of certain gospel truths: the dignity of the human person, greater respect for human rights, an overdue recognition of the equal dignity of women, a rejection of violence as a means of resolving conflict?

6. But the affirmation of certain moral values is not yet the proclamation of Jesus Christ, the one mediator between God and men (cf. 1 Tm 2:5). Our age needs to hear the revealed truth about God, about

man, and about the human condition. The moment is right for kerygma. The pastoral challenge of the Great Jubilee is to proclaim with renewed vigor "Jesus Christ, the one Savior of the world, yesterday, today, and forever" (cf. Heb 13:8). And the Catholic community in the United States is called to do so in a cultural climate, many of whose most powerful elements doubt the existence of objective, absolute truth and reject the very idea of authoritative teaching. The challenge of radical skepticism can lead to the assumption that the Church is marginal to contemporary life. Accepting this assumption, in turn, can lead to the notion that Catholicism, and indeed Christianity as a whole, is merely one form among many of the generic human reality called "religion."

This is not the message of the Second Vatican Council, which boldly proclaimed the centrality for human history of Jesus Christ and the essential mission of the Church to preach the Gospel to all nations: for "there is no other name under heaven given among men by which we must be saved" (Acts 4:12 [RSV]). The Church is sent to the world with a proposal, and the evangelical proposal we make is that the world can understand its history and its aspirations most adequately, most truthfully, through the Gospel. If this is the truth we proclaim, then the Church is never marginal, even when she seems weak in the eyes of the world.

Faced with a modernity which has lost the capacity to fulfill the noble aspiration it set out to realize—the complete liberation of man, of every man and every woman—the Church remains a witness to the full meaning of human freedom. A new phase in the history of freedom is opening up, and in these circumstances it is necessary that the Church, especially through her pastors, teach and evince that "the liberating capacities of science, technology, work, economics and political activity will only produce results if they find their inspiration and measure in the truth and love which are stronger than suffering: the truth and love revealed to men by Jesus Christ" (Congregation for the Doctrine of the Faith, *Instruction on Christian Freedom and Liberation*, no. 24, March 22, 1986).

The challenge is enormous, but the time is right. For other culture-forming forces are exhausted, implausible, or lacking in intellectual resources adequate to satisfy the human yearning for genuine liberation—even if those forces still manage to exercise a powerful attraction, especially through the media. The great achievement of the council is to have positioned the Church to engage modernity with the truth about the human condition given to us in Jesus Christ, who is the answer to the question that is every human life. A bishop's task is none other than this: to be a convincing witness to and a courageous teacher of the truth that makes man free (cf. Jn 8:42).

7. Dear brother bishops: At the Last Supper, Jesus challenged and encouraged his disciples: "Whoever loves me will keep my word, and my Father will love him, and we will come to him and make our dwelling with him" (Jn 14:23 [NAB]). We know that the Spirit dwells in the midst of the Church and leads the faithful to an ever more profound understanding of God's word, because Christ told his disciples that the Spirit "will teach you everything and remind you of all that [I] told you" (Jn 14:26 [NAB]). May the Spirit always assist you in fulfilling the task which the Council committed above all to the Church's pastors: that of communicating the truth and grace of Christ to the men and women of today's world (cf. *Ad Gentes*, no. 2; *Redemptoris Missio*, no. 1).

I commend to the intercession of Mary, mother of the Church and patroness of the United States, the joys and difficulties of your ministry, and the needs and hopes of your local churches and of the whole Catholic community in your country. To each of you and to all the priests, religious, and laity of your dioceses, I cordially impart my apostolic blessing.

FROM THE VATICAN, FEBRUARY 27, 1998

Joannes Paulus II

GREETING
OF THE BISHOPS
Region III

Most Holy Father:

It is with joy and fraternal affection that we, the bishops of Pennsylvania and New Jersey, extend to you our warm greetings and prayerful best wishes. We also bring the greetings, affection, and fervent prayers of our devoted priests, deacons, religious, and lay faithful.

The apostle Paul, a few years after his call from the Risen Lord, "did go up to Jerusalem to visit Cephas and stayed with him for fifteen days" (Gal 1:18 [NRSV]). So also do we come to Rome to visit with Your Holiness, the successor of Peter, and to be with you this week. We have come to be with you not primarily out of a sense of canonical obligation but more because of a holy desire to manifest our ecclesial communion with you—a communion filled with love and gratitude.

Fourteen years after his first visit with Peter, the apostle Paul returned to Jerusalem and set down for scrutiny the Gospel he was preaching to the Gentiles, "all this," as he wrote to the Galatians, "in private conference with the leaders, to make sure the course I was pursuing, or had pursued, was not useless" (Gal 2:1-2 [NAB 1970]). Holy Father, we have already presented our quinquennial reports setting down the diversity of persons, activities, and institutions through which we strive to preach the Gospel today in our particular churches. In our communion with you, like Paul, we submit our reports to you and the dicasteries of the Holy See for examination to make sure the course we are pursuing is not useless.

Humbled as we are to have been chosen by God to be successors of the apostles and as a visible expression of our ecclesial communion with them, we have come also to venerate the tombs of the apostles Peter and Paul.

These three components of our *Ad Limina* visit reflect that communion that unites in a wondrous and mysterious spiritual dynamic all of us bishops with Your Holiness and all of our particular churches with the See of Rome.

Most Holy Father, our ecclesial communion with you is also filled with immense gratitude. In this year marking the twentieth anniversary of your pontificate, we thank you for all your self-sacrificing service as our Supreme Pontiff.

We are grateful for your momentous encyclicals, the *Catechism of the Catholic Church,* and the many other vehicles of teaching, through which Your Holiness has strengthened the truths of the Catholic faith, comforted the hearts and minds of the faithful, and built up the ecclesial communion of faith and holiness.

We are also most grateful for the expression of communion that was uniquely manifested and strengthened among the bishops and particular churches of the new world at the Synod for America last year.

We thank you, Most Holy Father, for the total surrender of yourself to the mission of personally bringing to all people in every nation the joyful announcement of Christ our Savior. In a special way do we thank and admire you for your fruitful and courageous trip recently made to Cuba. Truly, you are Christ on earth visiting "all the towns and villages, teaching . . . , proclaiming the gospel of the kingdom, and curing every disease and illness" (Mt 9:35 [NAB]).

Most Holy Father, in answer to your call and under your guidance, we journey in communion with you and the whole Church toward the third millennium. With you, we also are confident that, in God's providence, the new millennium will bring a "new springtime" for the Church.

Your Holiness, we humbly ask for your apostolic blessing upon us and our faithful. We pledge our loyalty and obedience to you as well as the assurance of our prayers. We pray that Mary, the mother of the Church, will always strengthen, protect, and comfort you.

CARDINAL ANTHONY BEVILACQUA
ARCHBISHOP OF PHILADELPHIA

ADDRESS OF
POPE JOHN PAUL II
Region III

Dear Cardinal Bevilacqua,
Dear Brother Bishops:

1. "Grace to you and peace from God our Father and the Lord Jesus Christ" (Rom 1:7 [NAB]). Continuing this series of *Ad Limina* visits by the bishops of the United States, I welcome you, the bishops of Pennsylvania and New Jersey. I entrust the outcome of our prayer and meetings to the grace of the Holy Spirit, who "down the centuries has drawn from the treasures of the Redemption achieved by Christ and given new life to human beings" (*Dominum et Vivificantem*, no. 53). The Spirit is now preparing the Church for the Great Jubilee, a time to hear anew and answer ever more decisively the call to open our hearts to the Gospel, to embrace its saving message, and to allow it to transform our lives. Approaching the jubilee, the shepherds of God's people have a fresh opportunity to speak out and tell the men and women of today that God has indeed come among us and that the Gospel is "the power of God for salvation to every one who has faith" (Rom 1:16 [RSV]). Let us pray that the Holy Spirit will further enlighten our minds regarding the "hour" that we are living and regarding the opportunities and responsibilities which this "hour" entails for the future of the Church and of society.

2. As I mentioned to the first group of bishops from your country, the reception given to the teachings of the Second Vatican Council, and the renewal of the Church envisioned by the council, will be the guid-

ing light of our reflections during this series of visits *Ad Limina Apostolorum*. Many Catholics today have no personal recollection of the council. But those of us who had the marvelous opportunity to take part in it experienced it as a time of extraordinary spiritual dynamism and growth. The council brought us into close and tangible contact with the wealth of nineteen centuries of holiness, doctrine, and service to the human family; it revealed to us the unity and diversity of the Catholic community throughout the world; it taught us openness to our Christian brothers and sisters, to the followers of other religions, to mankind's joys and hopes, griefs and anxieties. It is clear that in his providence, God wanted to prepare the Church for a new springtime of the Gospel—for the beginning of the next Christian millennium—through the extraordinary grace of the council.

Among the teachings which the council has bequeathed to us, none has had so far-reaching an influence on the Catholic community as a whole, and on our own lives as priests and bishops, as the Church's reflection on herself, *ad intra* and *ad extra*, in the *Dogmatic Constitution on the Church (Lumen Gentium)* and the *Pastoral Constitution on the Church in the Modern World (Gaudium et Spes)*. How deeply has the council's vision of the Church penetrated the life of our Christian communities? What must be done to ensure that the whole Church enters the next millennium with a clearer awareness of her own mystery, with fuller confidence in her unique importance for the human family, with ardent commitment to her mission?

3.   As bishops, we have an urgent responsibility to help God's people to understand and appreciate the profound mystery of the Church: to see her above all as the community in which we meet the living God and his merciful love. It must be our pastoral objective to create a more intense awareness of the fact that God, who intervenes in history at times of his choosing, in the fullness of time sent his Son, born of a woman, for the salvation of the world (cf. Gal 4:4). This is the

great truth of human history: that the history of salvation has entered the history of the world, making it a history filled with God's presence and punctuated by events overflowing with meaning for the people God calls to be his own. The redemptive work of the Son continues in the Church and through the Church. Indeed, from the beginning God "planned to assemble in the Holy Church all those who would believe in Christ" (*Lumen Gentium*, no. 2). In this transcendent, theological sense, the Church is the goal of all things: for God created the world in order to communicate his own infinite goodness and to draw his beloved creatures into communion with himself, a communion brought about by the *convocation* of all in Christ. This convocation is the Church (cf. *Catechism of the Catholic Church*, no. 760). "Just as God's will is creation and is called 'the world,' so his intention is the salvation of men, and it is called 'the Church'" (Clement of Alexandria, *Paedagogus*, 1, 6, 27).

4. The fundamental truth about the Church which the council fathers sought to underline is that she is "the kingdom of Christ now present in mystery" (*Lumen Gentium*, no. 3). Christ's disciples are "in the world" without being "of the world" (cf. Jn 17:16); so they are obviously affected by the economic, social, political, and cultural processes which determine how peoples and societies live and act. Thus, on her pilgrim journey through history, the Church adapts to changing circumstances while always remaining the same, in fidelity to her Lord, to his revealed word and to "what has been handed on" under the guidance of the Holy Spirit. In the post-conciliar period we have been called to serve God's people in the midst of profound social change. The rapidity of change in the thirty years since the council, and the tendency of western cultures to confine religious convictions within the private sphere, has made it difficult in some cases for Catholics to "receive" the council's teaching on the Church's unique nature and mission. The cultural history of the United States has had a particular impact on how

Catholics have perceived the Church in recent decades. It is necessary to remind everyone that, precisely because the Church is a "mystery," her reality can never be fully captured by sociological or political categories or analyses.

Following the lead of Pope Pius XII in his encyclical *Mystici Corporis*, and after a period in which ecclesiology tended to focus primarily on the Church as an institution, the Second Vatican Council sought to deepen appreciation of the Church as the sacrament of encounter with the living Christ. As shepherds of souls, we must ask ourselves to what degree the call of *Lumen Gentium* to a more profound sense of the interior mystery of the Church has been heard. Or have Catholics sometimes succumbed to the temptation, widespread in modern western culture, to judge the Church in predominantly political terms? It was surely not the council's intention to "politicize" the Church so that every issue became susceptible to a political label. On the contrary, it was precisely to broaden and deepen our faith in and experience of the Church as a communion that the council fathers described the Church through that marvelous array of biblical images we find in *Lumen Gentium* 5 and 6, rather than in the institutional categories to which they were accustomed.

Now, more than thirty years after *Lumen Gentium* and *Gaudium et Spes*, we have sufficient perspective to see that while the fruits of the council are manifold and everywhere there are signs that the council has brought a new steadfastness in the faith, new signs of holiness, and a new love of the Church, there are still some tendencies towards a reductive understanding of the Church. As a result, inadequate ecclesiologies, radically different from what the council and the subsequent magisterium have presented, have found their way into theological and catechetical works. In pastoral practice these have become the basis of a more or less horizontal and sociological view of ecclesial realities on the part of some sectors of Catholicism. We must, therefore, look again at our efforts to teach the richly textured ecclesiology of the council.

5. We can only truly appreciate what the Church is when we understand that every aspect of her being is shaped by the new relationship, the new covenant, which God established between himself and mankind through the cross of Christ. The mystery which envelops us is a mystery of communion, a sharing through grace in the life of the Father given us through Christ in the Holy Spirit. We should never cease to reflect on the call to enter into this intimate relationship of life and love with the Most Blessed Trinity. The whole purpose of our ministry is to lead others into this communion, which is not of our own making. We have to lead the faithful to understand that we do not enter into communion with God simply through a personal option in accordance with our private tastes; we do not join the Church as we join some voluntary association. Rather, we are incorporated into the body of Christ through the grace of baptism and through full participation in all that constitutes the divine-human reality of the Church.

The community of Christ's followers is therefore above all a spiritual solidarity, the *communio sanctorum*. We are the pilgrim people of God, journeying to our heavenly home, assisted by the intercession of Mary and the saints who have preceded us. The Church embraces those who now see God as he is, and those who have died and are being purified. Perhaps our consciousness of this dimension of the Church's nature has decreased somewhat in recent years. More attention needs to be given to the intimate relationship between the Church on earth and the Church in heaven. Are younger Catholics sufficiently aware of the reality of Mary and the saints? Do the example and intercession of Mary and the saints sustain our people in responding to the universal vocation to holiness? Do we understand the Church's liturgy as a participation in the heavenly liturgy? Would a recovery of that understanding help to reinvigorate attendance at Sunday Mass?

6. The Church in the United States has been enriched by a great diversity of expressions of faith found among people of different ethnic

17

backgrounds. This rich diversity indicates that the Church is catholic in the full sense, embracing all peoples and cultures. Yet the Church, with all her different members, remains the one body of Christ. Diversity in the Church must serve the unity of the one faith, the one baptism (cf. Eph 4:5), so that "speaking the truth in love, we grow up in every way into him who is the head, into Christ, from whom the whole body, joined and knit together . . . build[s] itself up in love" (Eph 4:15-16 [NRSV]). Respect for a specific culture and tradition must always be accompanied by faithfulness to the essential truth of the Gospel as passed down in the teaching of the Church.

A particularly rich form of the diversity which builds up the body of Christ is found in the Eastern-rite churches present alongside the Latin church in many parts of your country. I am especially pleased to greet the archeparchs and eparchs taking part in this *Ad Limina* visit. The Eastern Catholics who live in the United States constitute a natural bridge between East and West. On the one hand they make known by direct experience the Christian East and, on the other, they contribute to the development of the Oriental churches in their countries of origin by witnessing to the acquisitions of the West and by providing spiritual and material support for people in their homeland. In order to fulfill this twofold task, it is essential that they maintain and deepen the sense of belonging to their specific ecclesial tradition, making use of the indications offered in the *Instruction for the Application of the Liturgical Prescriptions of the Code of Canons of the Oriental Churches*, issued by the Congregation for the Oriental Churches.

The pastors of the Eastern churches face new and demanding challenges in ensuring that the faithful recently arrived in the United States are properly integrated into their respective ecclesial communities. Serious consideration must also be given to ways of addressing the problems arising from the dispersal of the faithful, who continue to leave the areas where their community was traditionally present and where their ecclesial identity was more easily preserved, to live in other parts of the country.

These aspects highlight the great need for close collaboration between Latin and Oriental bishops in order to safeguard and guarantee the legitimate diversity which constitutes the richness of the Church's universality. I urge my brother bishops of the Latin rite to foster greater knowledge and appreciation of the eastern heritage which is an integral part of the Catholic expression of the faith. In this way all the faithful will have a more thorough understanding of the Christian experience, and the Catholic community will be capable of giving a more complete Christian response to the expectations of the men and women of today (cf. apostolic letter *Orientale Lumen*, no. 5).

7. Dear brother bishops, as we look forward in hope to the celebration of the Great Jubilee of the Year 2000, I pray that the priests, deacons, religious, and lay faithful of your dioceses will be inspired to grow in their love of the Church, and thus come into an ever more profound union with Christ the bridegroom. The most important aspect of our preparation for the celebration of the two thousandth anniversary of the incarnation is our response to the call to that holiness "without which no one shall see the Lord" (Heb 12:14 [NRSV]). For it is only in the grace of the Holy Spirit that God's people can truly challenge society by their untiring and courageous witness to the truth. Entrusting you and all those whom you serve to the maternal care of Mary, I cordially impart my apostolic blessing.

FROM THE VATICAN, MARCH 12, 1998

Joannes Paulus II

GREETING
OF THE BISHOPS
Region IV

Most Holy Father:

With so much joy, we, the bishops of the ecclesiastical provinces of Baltimore, Washington, Atlanta, and Miami, wish to express our profound gratitude and our filial devotion to Your Holiness. Our journey to the threshold of the apostles has led us here, to you, Holy Father, as the successor of Peter. You have welcomed us with love at the Lord's altar, where we celebrated his life-giving mysteries. You give us the opportunity to speak to you personally about our dioceses—about our projects and plans, our hopes and our anxieties. You also welcome us to your table, giving us yet another opportunity to converse with you and to experience your hospitality and concern.

Truly, Most Holy Father, we are confirmed and strengthened in our ministry by the instruction, guidance, and encouragement you offer us.

In a special and particular way we want to thank Your Holiness for the vision with which you lead us toward the third Christian millennium. From the very beginning of your pontificate, you have reminded us of the approaching two thousandth anniversary of Christ's birth and showed us its significance for the whole human family. At the same time, through the *Catechism of the Catholic Church* and countless pastoral endeavors, you have helped us strengthen the faith of those we serve in preparation for that new springtime of Christianity for which we all long.

One expression of that new springtime is World Youth Day. Last summer in Paris and previously in Manila and Denver, Your Holiness touched the minds and hearts of so many of our young people with the truth and love of Jesus. With you, we look forward to World Youth Day in Rome, in the year 2000.

A foremost expression of your pastoral care was the recent Synod on America. We are deeply grateful to Your Holiness for convoking that synod, which highlights the importance of concerted pastoral collaboration throughout the western hemisphere. I know, too, that I speak for all the bishops here present in thanking Your Holiness for your recent visit to Cuba. It has brought so much hope to the people of that country, to the many Cubans living in the United States, and to all people of goodwill who cherish human dignity and freedom.

Finally, we know that Your Holiness is preparing to journey to Nigeria. Your pastoral concern for the Church in Africa also strengthens our ministry to the growing number of African immigrants in our midst and to all those Americans who proudly claim their African heritage. May God protect you on your forthcoming journey.

As we strive to proclaim the Gospel of life in a culture which increasingly disregards the value of the lives of the unborn, the elderly, and the seriously ill, we are strengthened and encouraged by your courage and love.

Most Holy Father, we commend Your Holiness to the loving protection of Mary, the Immaculate Mother of God, patroness of our country. We affirm once more our love and loyalty and humbly ask you now for your apostolic blessing for us all and those whom we serve.

CARDINAL JAMES A. HICKEY
ARCHBISHOP OF WASHINGTON

ADDRESS OF
POPE JOHN PAUL II

Region IV

Dear Cardinal Hickey and Cardinal Keeler,
Dear Brother Bishops:

1. I warmly welcome you, the pastors of the ecclesiastical
provinces of Baltimore, Washington, Atlanta, and Miami. Your visit *Ad
Limina* is a time of grace as you pray at the tombs of the apostles Peter
and Paul, who fearlessly proclaimed the good news of salvation to the
point of martyrdom. In entrusting to them your pastoral mission of
preaching the "unsearchable riches of Christ" and of making known
"the plan of the mystery hidden for ages in God who created all things"
(Eph 3:8-9 [RSV]), may you feel reassured that you are not alone in
your task; the Lord provides the strength and the means necessary for
you to fulfill his command: "preach the gospel to the whole creation"
(Mk 16:15 [RSV]).

In my meetings with the first two groups of bishops from your
country, we have reflected together on the reception in your country of
the great grace of the Second Vatican Council. In those reflections I
referred to two essential elements of your episcopal ministry in the cultural context of the United States. First, because the message we preach
is God's wisdom, not our own, everything in the life of the Church
must correspond to "the truth that has been entrusted to you by the
Holy Spirit who dwells within us" (2 Tm 1:14 [RSV]). Secondly, the
purpose of our ministry is to lead the members of the Church into a living communion with God and with one another. That *communio*,

according to the Council, is the very heart of the Church's understanding of herself.

In this meeting, I would like to reflect with you on the truth that the pilgrim Church is missionary by her very nature, for the universal community of Christ's followers, present in and living through the particular churches, is the continuation in time of the eternal mission of the Son and of the Holy Spirit (cf. *Ad Gentes*, no. 2). As the whole Church prepares for the Great Jubilee of the Year 2000, I am confident that you will seek to renew among your communities a vital, dynamic sense of the Church's mission, so that this time of grace may be a new springtime for the Gospel. This is the hope and determination which inspired the recent Special Assembly for America of the Synod of Bishops, which issued a compelling call to conversion, communion, and solidarity. This same hope and determination inspires what you have written in your own national plan and strategy for Catholic evangelization in the United States, *Go and Make Disciples*, which is a significant and valid guide in your efforts "to bring about in all Catholics such an enthusiasm for their faith that, in living their faith in Jesus, they freely share it with others" (loc. cit., I).

2. In that document you rightly insist that "evangelization can only happen when people accept the Gospel freely as the 'good news' it is meant to be, because of the power of the gospel message and the accompanying grace of Christ." Evangelization is the Church's effort to proclaim to everyone that God loves them, that he has given himself for them in Christ Jesus, and that he invites them to an unending life of happiness. Once this Gospel has been accepted as the "good news," it demands to be shared. All baptized Christians must commit themselves to evangelization, conscious that God is already at work in the minds and hearts of their listeners, just as he prompted the Ethiopian to ask for baptism when Philip told him "the good news of Jesus" (Acts 8:35 [RSV]). Evangelization is thus a part of the great mystery of God's self-

revelation to the world: It involves the human effort to preach the Gospel and the powerful work of the Holy Spirit in those who encounter its saving message. Since we are proclaiming a mystery, we are the servants of a supernatural gift, which surpasses anything our human minds are capable of fully grasping or explaining, yet which attracts by its own inner logic and beauty.

3. The spirit of the new evangelization should inspire every aspect of your teaching, instruction, and catechesis. These tasks involve a vital effort to come to a deeper understanding of the mysteries of faith and to find meaningful language with which to convince our contemporaries that they are called to newness of life through God's love. Since love can only be understood by someone who actually loves, the Christian mystery can only be effectively communicated by those who allow themselves to be genuinely possessed by God's love. Thus the passing on of the faith, according to the Church's tradition, needs to be carried out in a spiritual environment of friendship with God, rooted in a love which will one day find its fulfillment in the contemplation of God himself. Everyone has a part to play in this great effort. Your task is to inspire priests, deacons, religious, and faithful to have the courage and the conviction to share their faith with others. By proclaiming the Gospel, Christians help others to satisfy the yearning for fullness of life and truth which exists in every human heart.

4. The parish will necessarily be the center of the new evangelization, and thus parish life must be renewed in all its dimensions. During the parish visitations I undertook as archbishop of Krakow, I always made an effort to stress that the parish is not an accidental collection of Christians who happen to live in the same neighborhood. Rather, because the parish makes present and in a sense incarnates the mystical body of Christ, the threefold *munus* (office) of Christ as prophet, priest, and king must be exercised there. Thus the parish must be a place

where, through worship in communion of doctrine and life with the bishop and with the universal Church, the members of Christ's body are formed for evangelization and works of Christian love. A parish will be involved in many activities. But none is as vital or as community-forming as the Sunday celebration of the Lord's day and his eucharist (cf. *Catechism of the Catholic Church*, no. 2177). Through regular and fervent reception of the sacraments, God's people come to know the fullness of the Christian dignity that is theirs by baptism; they are elevated and transformed. Through careful listening to the word of Scripture and sound instruction in the faith they are enabled to experience their lives, and the life of the parish, as a dynamic sharing in the history of salvation. That experience, in turn, becomes a powerful motive for evangelization.

Everything you do to ensure the correct and worthy celebration of the eucharist and the other sacraments, precisely because it leads the faithful to a deep and transforming encounter with God, builds up the Church in her inner life and as the visible sign of salvation for the world. Preaching and catechesis should emphasize that the grace of the sacraments is what enables us to live in accordance with the demands of the Gospel. Adoration of the eucharist outside of the Mass permits a deeper appreciation of the gift that Christ makes to us in his body and blood in the holy sacrifice of the altar. Encouragement of frequent recourse to the sacrament of penance increases the spiritual maturity of all parishioners as they strive to commit themselves to witnessing to the truth of the Gospel in private and public life.

5. The strength of parish life in your country can be judged above all from the way families pass on the faith to each succeeding generation, and from the impressive and essential system of Catholic schools that you and your predecessors have built and sustained at great sacrifice. As a priest and bishop I have always been convinced that ministry to families is an extremely important dimension of the Church's evan-

gelizing task since "the family itself is the first and most appropriate place for teaching the truths of the faith, the practice of Christian virtues, and the essential values of human life."[1] Catholic schools for their part must have a specific Catholic identity, and those who administer them and teach in them have a responsibility to uphold and communicate the truths, values, and ideals which constitute a truly Catholic education.

Many of your parishes have committed themselves to winning inactive Catholics back to the practice of the faith and to reaching out to all those in search of the truth of the Gospel. These efforts are a profound expression of the essential missionary nature of the Church which should mark every parish community. I am aware of the complexities of parish life in the United States and of the burden of work borne by priests, deacons, religious, and laity as they face the daily challenge of inspiring God's people to live the Gospel more fully and build a society imbued with Christian values. Be close to all those who work in parishes, sustaining them with your prayer and wise counsel, endeavoring to create in everyone the *sensus ecclesiae*, a vivid sense of what belonging to the Church means in practical terms.

6. At the recent special session for America of the Synod of Bishops, the bishops called on all the faithful to be "evangelists of the new millennium," by witnessing to the faith through lives of holiness, kindness to all, charity to those in need, and solidarity with all the oppressed.[2] In living the faith and communicating it to others in a culture that tends to treat religious convictions as merely a personal "option," evangelization's only point of departure is Jesus Christ, "the way, and the truth, and the life" (Jn 14:6 [RSV]), the answer to the question that is every human life. As you lead the Church in the United States in preparation for the Great Jubilee, help everyone in the Catholic community to understand that we know, love, worship, and serve God, not as a response to some psychological "need," but as a duty whose

fulfillment is an expression of man's highest dignity and the source of man's most profound happiness. An essential part of your ministry must be to help all sectors of the Catholic community find greater certainty about what the Church actually teaches, and greater serenity in confronting the many issues which—often needlessly—cause division and polarization among those who should be of one mind and heart (cf. Acts 2:44). As the recent synod said, all must be encouraged "to turn from hesitant and wary steps, to walk in joy with Jesus on the road to everlasting life."[3]

Because Christians have come to know Christ and the liberating force of his Gospel, they have a particular responsibility to contribute to the renewal of culture. In this task, which pertains in a special way to the laity, Christ's followers should not cease to make present in all areas of public life the light which Christ's teaching sheds on the human condition. In contemporary culture there is often a weakening of the sense of the innate dependence of all human existence on the Creator, the capacity of the human mind to know the truth, and the validity of the universal and unchanging moral norms which guide all people in the fulfillment of their human vocation. When freedom is detached from the truth about the human person and from the moral law inscribed in human nature, then society and its democratic form of life are imperiled. For if freedom is not linked to truth and ordered to goodness, "the ground is laid for society to be at the mercy of the unrestrained will of individuals or the oppressive totalitarianism of public authority" (*Evangelium Vitae*, no. 96). In proclaiming the truths about the human person, human community, and human destiny that they know from revelation and reason, Christians make an indispensable contribution to sustaining a free society, a society in which freedom nurtures genuine human development.

7. Dear brother bishops, as we approach the next Christian millennium, encourage all Catholics in the United States to deepen their com-

mitment to the Church's evangelizing mission. Lead them by your example, your conviction, and your teaching. I pray that the Holy Spirit will enlighten you and help you to inspire your people, so that the hearts of the faithful will burn more brightly with love for Christ and a desire to make him better known. Entrusting you and all the priests, religious, and laity of your dioceses to Mary, Mother of the Redeemer, I cordially impart my apostolic blessing.

FROM THE VATICAN, MARCH 17, 1998

Joannes Paulus II

Notes

1. Address at Our Lady of Guadalupe Plaza, San Antonio, September 13, 1987, no. 4.

2. Cf. Message to America, no. 30.

3. Message to America, no. 37.

GREETING
OF THE BISHOPS

Region V

Most Holy Father:

The bishops of Region V of the National Conference of Catholic Bishops in the United States are deeply grateful for this opportunity to experience the blessing of unity, affirmation, and renewal that is ours on the occasion of this *Ad Limina* visit to Rome. Your own generous availability in time, attention, and affection is truly the centerpiece of a tradition that touches us personally, and through us the Church of the central and Gulf southland of our country. With joy we celebrate and share in your task as successor of St. Peter to "strengthen your brothers" (cf. Lk 22:32), an intention which has been uppermost in our eucharistic liturgies at the tombs of the apostles.

Coming as pilgrims "in service to the Gospel" we wish to thank you for your own apostolic journeys worldwide in that same service, continuing a practice most recently begun by your predecessor Pope Paul VI. Your return, within the fortnight, from a pastoral visit to the Church in Nigeria is but the latest witness to your "care for all the churches." The quinquennium past has seen like evidence of your pastoral solicitude in convening the Synod for America, a service to the faith in our own hemisphere; the *Catechism of the Catholic Church* for the Church universal; and your continuing initiatives for the celebration of the Great Jubilee of the Year 2000 proclaiming anew the centrality of Jesus Christ as the Lord of history. In a special way, Most Holy Father, we, who come from a region of five states, Kentucky, Tennessee,

Louisiana, Mississippi, and Alabama with a combined population of 19,400,122 wherein Catholics number slightly more than two million, have received with gratitude the encyclical *Ut Unum Sint* for the sake of deepening relationships of understanding, trust, and love with so many of our friends and neighbors who are not of the Catholic faith.

Finally, Your Holiness, we await with anticipation, for the effectiveness of our own ministry of preaching and teaching, your reflections on certain themes of Vatican Council II "in an effort to discern how best we can ensure that all God wishes for the Church will become a reality."[1] In union with Peter we are joined with him in proclaiming the fullness of the apostolic message of God's love for all of humankind. We pledge ourselves to return to our particular churches with this perennial truth as the heart of an evangelization that is new in method, expression, and zeal in keeping with the needs of our times. To this end, Holy Father, we ask your prayers and blessing that, in the words of Bishop Samuel Jacobs of Alexandria, La., our deeds "be a witness of love of the Father for all mankind."[2] As an example of such witness we commend to you and congratulate our brother, Joseph Lawson Howze, bishop of Biloxi, who this year celebrates twenty-five years of ministry as bishop in the state of Mississippi.

MOST REV. OSCAR H. LIPSCOMB
ARCHBISHOP OF MOBILE

Notes

1. John Paul II, "Address to the Bishops of the United States, Region II," *Ad Limina Addresses* (Washington, D.C.: United States Catholic Conference, 1998), p. 4.

2. Bishop Samuel Jacobs, "How Must Catholics Evangelize? Evangelization and the Power of the Holy Spirit," *Pope John Paul II and the New Evangelization*, Ralph Martin and Peter Williamson, eds. (San Francisco: Ignatius Press, 1995), p. 62.

ADDRESS OF
POPE JOHN PAUL II
Region V

Dear Brother Bishops:

1. Following the visits of other groups of bishops of the United States, I now warmly welcome you, the bishops of the ecclesiastical provinces of Louisville, Mobile, and New Orleans. Through you I greet each member of the dioceses in which the Holy Spirit has made you overseers to care for the Church of God (cf. Acts 20:28). In a special way I thank God for the bonds of communion which unite us in the episcopal ministry at the service of his holy people. The Church's experience since the Second Vatican Council illustrates how important the ministry of the bishop is for the renewal which the council advocated and for the new evangelization which must be undertaken on the threshold of the third Christian millennium. And so I propose to reflect today on some of the more fundamental aspects of this ministry of ours, which comes to us from the apostles "in a sequence running back to the beginning" (*Lumen Gentium*, no. 20).

2. In your document *The Teaching Ministry of the Diocesan Bishop*, you drew attention to an important truth: the episcopal ministry is a crucial part of God's saving work in human history. It cannot be reduced to "a variation of the common human need for organization and authority" (loc. cit., 1, A, 1). It is in fact by the mandate and command of Christ that bishops teach "the unchanging faith of the Church as it is to be understood and lived today" (ibid., 1, A, 2). This duty can only be

understood and fulfilled in the context of a bishop's personal adherence to the faith. In fact, the Lord's mandate to his apostles to teach in his name is not without a connection to a profound act of faith on their part: the act of faith by which the apostles, with Peter, recognized that Jesus was "the Messiah, the Son of the living God" (Mt 16:16 [NRSV]). That same profession of faith in Christ must always be at the heart of a bishop's life and ministry.

In his diocese the bishop declares the faith of the Church with the authority which derives from his episcopal ordination and from communion with the College of Bishops under its head (cf. *Lumen Gentium*, no. 22). His task is to teach in a pastoral way, illuminating modern problems with the light of the Gospel and helping the faithful to live full Christian lives amid the challenges of our times (cf. *Directory on the Pastoral Ministry of Bishops*, no. 56). In applying the Gospel to new issues while safeguarding the authentic interpretation of the Church's teaching, the bishop ensures that the local Church abides in the truth which saves and liberates. All this requires that the bishop be a man of firm supernatural faith and steadfast loyalty to Christ and his Church.

3. Our teaching carries with it a great responsibility since it is "endowed with the authority of Christ" (*Lumen Gentium*, no. 25); yet we must teach and preach with great humility since we are the servants of the word, not its masters. If we are to be effective teachers, we must allow our entire existence to be transformed by prayer and the continuous submission of ourselves to God in imitation of Christ himself. To satisfy the thirst among the people of God for the truth of the Gospel, we bishops should take heed of St. Charles Borromeo's words to his priests at his last synod: "Is your duty preaching and teaching? Concentrate carefully on what is essential to fulfill that office fittingly. Make sure in the first place that your life and conduct are sermons in themselves" (*Liturgy of the Hours*, Feast of St. Charles).

Preaching the gospel message effectively requires constant personal prayer, study, reflection, and consultation with knowledgeable advisers. Commitment to the study and scholarship demanded by the *munus episcopale* is crucial in guarding "the truth that has been entrusted to you by the Holy Spirit who dwells within us" (2 Tm 1:14 [RSV]) and in proclaiming it with power "in and out of season" (2 Tm 4:2 [RSV]). Since the bishop has a personal responsibility to teach the faith, he needs time to assimilate the content of the Church's tradition and magisterium prayerfully. Likewise, he should be familiar with helpful developments in theology, in biblical studies, and in moral reflection on social issues. I know from my own experience as a diocesan bishop the many demands that are made on a bishop's time. Yet that experience convinced me that it is essential to make time, intentionally, for study and reflection. For it is only through study and reflection and prayer that the bishop, working with his collaborators, can guide and govern in a truly Christian and ecclesial manner, always asking himself: "What is the truth of faith that sheds light on the problem we are addressing?" Thus the bishop today may need to reorganize the way in which he exercises his episcopal office in order to attend to what is fundamental in his ministry.

4. The Great Jubilee of the Year 2000 calls us to redouble our efforts to preach the Gospel in response to the deep-rooted desire for spiritual truth that characterizes our times. This "hour" of evangelization makes special demands on bishops. In *The Teaching Ministry of the Diocesan Bishop*, you identified the qualities which render a bishop's teaching effective. Through his pastoral experience, study, reflection, judgment, and prayer, he must make the salvific truth his own so that he can communicate the fullness of faith and encourage the faithful in living according to the demands of the Gospel. The bishop is charged with transmitting the faith he has received; hence he must see his teaching as a humble service to the word of God and the Church's tradition. Being

ready to suffer for the sake of the Gospel (cf. 2 Tm 1:8), he must proclaim the truth courageously, even if this means challenging socially acceptable opinion. The bishop should teach frequently and constantly, preaching homilies, writing pastoral letters, giving conferences, and making use of the media, in such a way that he is seen to teach the faith and so bear public witness to the Gospel. Moreover, his teaching should be marked by charity, in accordance with Paul's words to Timothy: "the Lord's servant must not be quarrelsome but kindly to every one, an apt teacher, forbearing, correcting his opponents with gentleness" (2 Tm 2:24-25 [RSV]).

5. "Tend the flock of God that is your charge" (1 Pt 5:2 [RSV]). Any reflection on your responsibility for the pastoral governance of that part of God's people entrusted to you "as the vicars and ambassadors of Christ" (*Lumen Gentium*, no. 27) must begin from careful consideration of the example of Christ himself, the Good Shepherd, our supreme model. In the recent Special Assembly for America of the Synod of Bishops, many pastors raised questions about the example of their own lives and ministry, knowing that the people of God will heed their voice and respond if their witness is perceived as authentic. In the Synod Hall we heard the call for bishops as individuals and as a body to become more simple, with the simplicity of Jesus and of the Gospel—a simplicity which consists in being immersed in the essential things of the Father (cf. Lk 2:49).

In order to meet the needs of modern times, dioceses have frequently developed complex structures and a variety of diocesan offices which provide assistance in the exercise of pastoral government. As bishops, however, you must be careful to safeguard the personal nature of your governance, devoting much time to knowing the strengths and weaknesses of your dioceses, the faithful's expectations and needs, their traditions and charisms, the social context in which they live, and the long-term problems which need to be addressed. This means ensuring that the structures necessary today in leading a diocese do not impede the very thing they are meant to facilitate: a bishop's contact with his people and his role as an evangelist. In the synod it was pointed out that it is all too easy today for a bishop to yield his evangelizing and catechizing responsibility to others and become a captive of his own administrative obligations. Since our ministry is always directed to the building up of the body of the Church in truth and holiness (cf. *Lumen Gentium*, no. 27), the exercise of episcopal authority is never a mere administrative necessity but a witness to the truth about God and man revealed in Jesus Christ and a service for the good of all. In order to lead people to the fullness of Jesus Christ we must in fact "do the work of the evangelist" (2 Tm 4:5 [RSV]). No other task is as urgent as this.

6. In a special way a diocesan bishop must make every effort to maintain a close relationship with his priests, a relationship characterized by charity and concern for their spiritual and material well-being. In promoting an atmosphere of mutual confidence and trust, he is to be a teacher, father, friend, and brother to them (cf. *Directory for the Pastoral Ministry of Bishops*, no. 107). In this way the juridical bond of obedience between priest and bishop is animated by that supernatural charity which existed between Christ and his disciples. This pastoral charity and spirit of communion between bishop and priests is vital for the effectiveness of the apostolate. Likewise, it must be the bishop's special care to reach out to young men whom Christ is calling to share in his priesthood through the ordained ministry. Experience has shown that when the local bishop takes this responsibility seriously, there is no "vocation shortage." Young men want to be called to radical self-giving, and the bishop, insofar as he is the one principally responsible for the continuation of Christ's saving mission in the world, is the one who can repeat Christ's words with authority: "Follow me, and I will make you fishers of men" (Mt 4:19 [RSV]).

The relation between the bishop and members of religious communities should likewise be inspired by his esteem for the consecrated life and his commitment to making the various charisms known in the local Church, again with an eye to inviting young people to live out their baptismal grace by generously embracing the evangelical counsels. Moreover, since the council we are all more aware of the need to recognize, safeguard, and promote the dignity, rights, and duties of the faithful. It is essential that their service to the ecclesial community, their counsel, and their efforts to bring the Church's teaching to bear on contemporary culture through the transformation of intellectual, political, and economic life be appreciated and encouraged by the bishop and his close collaborators.

7. The aftermath of the Second Vatican Council witnessed the development of episcopal conferences as instruments for exercising that collegiality among bishops which springs from ordination and hierarchical communion. The conference exists to foster the sharing of pastoral experience and to allow for a common approach to various questions that arise in the life of the Church in a particular region or country. Your recent decision to study the structure and functions of your conference suggests that you recognize a need to rethink its operations so that they may better serve the pastoral and evangelical purposes that give the conference its unique meaning.

Among other things, this means that the episcopal conference must find a way to be truly effective without weakening the teaching and pastoral authority which belongs to bishops alone. Its administrative structures must not become ends in themselves but always remain instruments of the great tasks of evangelization and ecclesial service. Special care must be taken to ensure that the conference functions as an ecclesial body and not as an institution reflecting the management models of secular society. In this way each bishop will be enabled to bring his unique gifts to bear on the discussions and decisions of the conference. The bishop's duty to teach, sanctify, and govern is in fact a personal one which cannot be surrendered to others.

8. We can never remind ourselves too often that the pastors of the Church are personally responsible for passing on the light and joy of the faith. To say this is immediately to confront the question of our own faith and conviction. Your *Ad Limina* visit, with your prayer at the tombs of the apostles Peter and Paul, offers a grace-filled occasion to remember how essential to your witness is your own relationship to Christ and the seriousness of your personal quest for holiness. The vitality of your local churches and the well-being of the universal Church is first and always a gift of the Holy Spirit. But that gift is not independent of the ardent prayer and self-giving pastoral charity of the bishops, as individuals and as a body. In our weaknesses we need to be sustained by the grace of the Holy Spirit in order to be able to say without fear: "Lord, to whom shall we go? You have the words of eternal life; and we have believed, and have come to know, that you are the Holy One of God" (Jn 6:68, 69 [RSV]). On the two thousandth anniversary of the incarnation, may the Church—the bride—offer her Lord an episcopal college united and steadfast in faith, ardent in bearing witness to the Gospel of God's grace and dedicated to the ministration of the Spirit and of God's glorious power to make men just (cf. *Lumen Gentium*, no. 21).

Dear brothers, with these reflections on your ministry, I wish to encourage you in the grace and vocation that Christ has bestowed upon you. I pray for you as you go about your task of proclaiming the love of God and the mysteries of salvation to all, confident that the Holy Spirit will guide and fortify you. In gratitude for your work in preaching the word of God with unfailing patience and sound teaching (cf. 2 Tm 4:2), I commend you to the intercession of the Blessed Virgin Mary, *Sedes Sapientiae*, that she may sustain you in pastoral wisdom and bring joy and peace to your hearts. To you and the priests, religious, and lay faithful of your dioceses, I cordially impart my apostolic blessing.

FROM THE VATICAN, MARCH 30, 1998

Joannes Paulus II

GREETING
OF THE BISHOPS
Region VI

Your Holiness:

On behalf of the bishops of the states of Michigan and Ohio, I offer greetings of fraternal love and affection, the assurance of our prayers, and our desire to be your collaborators in the special work God has entrusted to you as the successor of St. Peter, "the perpetual and visible source and foundation of the unity of the bishops and the multitude of the faithful" (*Lumen Gentium*, no. 23).

We are humbled by the ministry confided to us to work as successors of the apostles. In you and your service of the Church universal, we find an outstanding example of how to fulfill our ministry. Your missionary zeal and untiring proclamation of the Gospel continue to be a challenge and an inspiration to us in our work. During these past two decades, with tireless energy and undaunted courage, you have shown us the way by proclaiming the Gospel of life and by encouraging us to be committed to the well-being of the Church in every part of the world.

We are most grateful for the recent experience of the Synod of America and your pastoral visit to Cuba, which has unleashed a fresh outpouring of the Holy Spirit not only for the people of Cuba but also in our own nation as well. Holy Father, you continue to open doors of hope for people everywhere as we prepare for the dawning of the third millennium of Christianity.

The Church in the states of Michigan and Ohio is using well these last years of the twentieth century to prepare for the Great Jubilee. Our church is strong and healthy, building on the rich ethnic heritage and diversity of all the cultural traditions that are woven together in our three hundred-year history of Christian faith. We continue to remember with gratitude and joy your second pastoral visit to the United States when, in the city of Detroit, you challenged us to global solidarity.

As bishops, following your own example, Holy Father, we have given a prime focus for our time and energy to proclaiming the dignity of every human life from the first moment of conception until its last natural breath. In every way possible, we have tried to use the preparation for the third millennium as an opportunity for a new evangelization of lifelong Catholics and as a means for raising questions of moral conversion in the wider society.

Thanks to the cooperative and generous spirit of our priests, religious, and laity, we are working with the Holy Spirit to renew our church from within and to make it more and more a sign of hope and healing for our fellow Christians, believers of other faith traditions, and those who are still struggling to hear the call of God.

In this month of May and in this year of the Holy Spirit, we ask, Holy Father, for your apostolic blessing for ourselves and for those that we serve: Like Mary and with Mary, may we be ever docile to the manifold gifts of God's Holy Spirit. May the Great Jubilee be a true celebration of Pentecost, and may God give you the grace and strength to continue to lead our Church into the new millennium.

CARDINAL ADAM J. MAIDA
ARCHBISHOP OF DETROIT

ADDRESS OF
POPE JOHN PAUL II
Region VI

Dear Cardinal Maida,
Dear Brother Bishops:

1. On the occasion of your *Ad Limina* visit, I welcome with great joy the fifth group of bishops from the United States, from the states of Michigan and Ohio. Your pilgrimage to the tombs of the apostles Peter and Paul provides a fresh opportunity to reflect on the witness which they gave *usque ad sanguinis effusionem* and expresses the profound bond of communion which exists between the bishops and the successor of Peter. These days are therefore a time of reflection on your own ministry as bishops and your special responsibility before Christ for the well-being of his body, the Church. May the example of the first witnesses and their intercession be a source of strength to you in preaching the Gospel, bearing in mind St. Paul's words to Timothy: "The aim of our charge is love that issues from a pure heart and a good conscience and sincere faith" (1 Tm 1:5 [RSV]).

In this series of *Ad Limina* talks, I have chosen to reflect on the opportunities presented by the Great Jubilee of the Year 2000 for evangelization in the light of the extraordinary grace which was and is the Second Vatican Council. At my last meeting with bishops from your country, I referred to the distinctive apostolic character of the bishop's own ministry and its importance for the spiritual renewal of the Christian community. Today I wish to mention the identity and mission of priests, your co-workers in the task of sanctifying the people of God and handing on the faith (cf. *Lumen Gentium*, no. 28). With immense gratitude, I think of all your priests whose lives are deeply marked by fidelity to Christ and generous dedication to their brothers and sisters. Alongside their brothers and sisters in the consecrated life, to whom I hope to dedicate a future reflection in this series, they are at the heart of the renewal which the Holy Spirit continually fosters in the Church.

2. Two years ago I celebrated my own fiftieth anniversary of ordination, and I can truly say that my experience of the priesthood has been a source of great joy to me throughout these years. Reflecting on the priesthood in *Gift and Mystery*, I emphasized two essential truths. The priestly vocation is a *mystery* of divine election, and therefore a *gift* which infinitely transcends the individual. As I look back, I am constantly reminded of the words of Jesus to his apostles: "You did not choose me, but I chose you and appointed you that you should go and bear fruit and that your fruit should abide" (Jn 15:16 [RSV]). In meditating on these words, a priest becomes more aware of the mysterious choice that God has made in calling him to this service, not because of his talents or merits but in virtue of God's "own purpose and the grace which he gave us" (2 Tm 1:9 [RSV]). It is vital for the life of the Church in your dioceses that you devote much attention to your priests and to the *quality* of their life and ministry. Through word and example you should constantly remind them that the priesthood is a special vocation which consists in being uniquely configured to Christ the high priest, the teacher, sanctifier, and shepherd of his people, through the imposition of hands and the invocation of the Holy Spirit in the sacrament of holy orders. It is not a career, nor does it mean belonging to a clerical caste. For this reason, "the priest must be conscious that his life is a mystery totally grafted onto the mystery of Christ and of the Church in a new and specific way and that this engages him totally in pastoral activity" (*Directory for the Life and Ministry of Priests*, no. 6). Thus the

priest's whole life is transformed so that he may *be Christ* for others: a convincing and efficacious sign of God's loving and saving presence. He should live the priesthood as a total gift of himself to the Lord. And if this gift is to be authentic, his thoughts, attitudes, activity, and relations with others must all show that he has truly put on the "mind of Christ" (cf. 1 Cor 2:16). With St. Paul he should be able to say, "It is no longer I who live, but Christ who lives in me; and the life I now live in the flesh I live by faith in the Son of God, who loved me and gave himself for me" (Gal 2:20 [RSV]). We should gratefully recognize the signs of a genuine renewal of the spirituality of the priesthood and foster a fresh blossoming of the authentic theological tradition of priestly life wherever it may have become obscured.

3. If bishops and priests are to be truly effective witnesses to Christ and teachers of the faith, they have to be men of prayer like Christ himself. Only by turning frequently and trustingly to God and seeking the guidance of the Holy Spirit can a priest fulfill his mission. Priests and seminarians preparing for the priesthood need to interiorize the fact that "an intimate bond exists between the priest's spiritual life and the exercise of his ministry" (*Pastores Dabo Vobis*, no. 24). Every priest is called to develop a great personal familiarity with the word of God, so that he may enter ever more completely into the Master's thought and strengthen his attachment to the Lord, his priestly model and guide (cf. General Audience, June 2, 1993, no. 4). A committed prayer life brings the gift of wisdom, with which "the Spirit leads the priest to evaluate all things in the light of the Gospel, helping him to read in his own experience and the experience of the Church the mysterious and loving plan of the Father" (Letter to Priests 1998, no. 5).

At a time when many demands are made on the priest's time and energies, it is important to emphasize that one of his first duties is to pray on behalf of the people entrusted to him. This is his privilege and his responsibility, for he has been ordained to represent his people before the Lord and to intercede on their behalf before the throne of grace (cf. General Audience, June 2, 1993, no. 5). In this regard, I would emphasize again the importance in priestly life of faithfully praying the liturgy of the hours, the public prayer of the Church, every day. While the faithful are invited to participate in this prayer, following Christ's recommendation to pray at all times without losing heart (cf. Lk 18:1), priests have received a special commission to celebrate the divine office, in which Christ himself prays with us and for us (cf. Letter to Priests 1984, no. 5). Indeed prayer for the needs of the Church and the individual faithful is so important that serious thought should be given to reorganizing priestly and parish life to ensure that priests have time to devote to this essential task, individually and in common. Liturgical and personal prayer, not the tasks of management, must define the rhythms of a priest's life, even in the busiest of parishes.

4. The celebration of the eucharist is the most important moment of the priest's day, the center of his life. Offering the sacrifice of the Mass, in which the unique sacrifice of Christ is made present and applied until he comes again, the priest ensures that the work of redemption continues to be carried out (cf. *Presbyterorum Ordinis*, no. 13). From this unique sacrifice, the priest's entire ministry draws its strength (cf. ibid., no. 2) and the people of God receive the grace to live truly Christian lives in the family and in society. It is important for bishops and priests not to lose sight of the intrinsic value of the eucharist, a value which is independent of the circumstances surrounding its celebration. For this reason, priests should be encouraged to celebrate Mass every day, even in the absence of a congregation, since it is an act of Christ and the Church (cf. ibid., no. 13; Code of Canon Law, c. 904).

In order that the eucharist may fully produce its grace in the life of your communities, specific attention also needs to be given to promoting the sacrament of penance. Priests are the special witnesses and ministers of God's mercy. At no other time can they be as close to the faithful as when they lead them to the crucified and forgiving Christ in this uniquely personal encounter (cf. *Redemptor Hominis*, no. 20). To be the minister of the sacrament of reconciliation is a special privilege for a priest who, acting in the person of Christ, is permitted to enter into the drama of another Christian life in a singular way. Priests should always be available to hear the confessions of the faithful, and to do so in a way that allows the penitent's particular situation to unfold and be reflected upon in the light of the Gospel. This fundamental task of the pastoral ministry, directed to intensifying the union of each individual with the Father of mercies, is a vital dimension of the Church's mission. It should be the subject of study and reflection in priests' gatherings and in courses of continuing formation. To cut oneself off from the sacrament of penance is to cut oneself off from an irreplaceable form of encounter with Christ. So, priests themselves should receive this sacrament regularly and in a spirit of genuine faith and devotion. In this way, the priest's own constant conversion to the Lord is strengthened, and the faithful see more clearly that reconciliation with God and the Church is necessary for authentic Christian living (cf. *Directory for the Life and Ministry of Priests*, no. 53).

5. As teachers of the faith, priests play a direct role in responding to the great challenge of evangelization facing the Church as we prepare to enter the third Christian millennium. The Gospel we preach is the truth about God and about man and the human condition: The people of our time want to hear this truth in all its fullness. Thus the Sunday homily requires careful preparation on the part of the priest, who is personally responsible for helping the faithful to see how the Gospel sheds light on the path of individuals and of society (cf. General Audience, April 21, 1993, no. 5). The *Catechism of the Catholic Church* is an excellent resource for preaching, and by using it priests will help their communities to grow in knowledge of the Christian mystery in all its inexhaustible richness, and so help them to be grounded in true holiness

and strengthened for witness and service (cf. Letter to Priests for Holy Thursday, April 8, 1993, no. 2).

The parish is a "family of families" and should be organized to support family life in every way possible. My own experience as a young priest in Krakow taught me how much the assistance that priests can give to young couples as they prepare for the responsibilities of married life is also of great benefit to their own priestly spirituality. Priests are called to a unique form of spiritual fatherhood and can come to a deeper appreciation of the meaning of being a "man for others" through their pastoral care of those striving to live out the requirements of self-giving and fruitful love in Christian marriage.

It is the priest's task to lead the faithful to spiritual maturity in Christ, so that they may respond to the call to holiness and fulfill their vocation to transform the world in the spirit of the Gospel (cf. *Christifideles Laici*, no. 36). In collaborating closely with the laity, priests must encourage them to see the Gospel as the principal force for the renewal of society—the vast and complex world of politics and economics, but also the world of culture, of the sciences and the arts, of international life, of the mass media (cf. *Evangelii Nuntiandi*, no. 70). A priest need not be an expert in all these things, but he should be an expert in discerning the "higher gifts" which the Holy Spirit abundantly pours out for the building of the kingdom (cf. 1 Cor 12:31), and he should help his people apply those gifts in advancing a civilization of love.

6. A bishop cannot fail to be personally involved in the promotion of vocations to the priesthood, and he needs to encourage the whole community of faith to play an active role in this work. "The time has come to speak courageously about priestly life as a priceless gift and a splendid and privileged form of Christian living" (*Pastores Dabo Vobis*, no. 39). Experience shows that when the invitation is made, the response is generous. A priest's pastoral contact with young people; his

closeness to them in their problems; his attitude of openness, benevolence, and availability—are all part of authentic youth ministry. A priest is a true spiritual guide when he helps young people to make important decisions about their lives, and especially when he helps them to answer the question: What does Christ want of me? More needs to be done to ensure that all priests are convinced of the fundamental importance of this aspect of the ministry. In the promotion and discernment of priestly vocations, there is no substitute for the presence of a committed, mature, and happy priest with whom young people can meet and talk.

7. As bishops, you must explain to the faithful why the Church does not have authority to ordain women to the ministerial priesthood, at the same time making clear why this is not a question of the equality of persons or of their God-given rights. The sacrament of holy orders and the ministerial priesthood are given by God as a gift: in the first place, to the Church; and then to the individual called by God. Thus ordination to the ministerial priesthood can never be claimed by anyone as a right; no one is "due" holy orders within the economy of salvation. That discernment belongs, finally, to the Church, through the bishop. And the Church ordains only on the basis of that ecclesial and episcopal discernment.

The Church's teaching that only men may be ordained to the ministerial priesthood is an expression of fidelity to the witness of the New Testament and the constant tradition of the Church of East and West. The fact that Jesus himself chose and commissioned men for certain specific tasks did not in any way diminish the human dignity of women (which he clearly intended to emphasize and defend); nor by doing so did he relegate women to a merely passive role in the Christian community. The New Testament makes it clear that women played a vital part in the early Church. The New Testament witness and the constant tradition of the Church remind us that the ministerial priesthood cannot be understood in sociological or political categories, as a matter of exercising "power" within the community. The priesthood of holy orders must be understood theologically, as one form of service in and for the Church. There are many forms of such service, as there are many gifts given by the same Spirit (1 Cor 12:4-11).

The churches—in particular the Catholic and Orthodox churches—which set sacramentality at the heart of the Christian life and the eucharist at the heart of sacramentality, are those which claim no authority to ordain women to the ministerial priesthood. Conversely, Christian communities more readily confer a ministerial responsibility on women the further they move away from a sacramental understanding of the Church, the eucharist, and the priesthood. This is a phenomenon that needs to be explored more deeply by theologians in collaboration with the bishops. At the same time, it is indispensable that you continue to pay attention to the whole question of how women's specific gifts are nurtured, accepted, and brought to fruition in the ecclesial community (cf. *Letter to Women*, nos. 11-12). The "genius" of women must be ever more a vital strength of the Church of the next millennium, just as it was in the first communities of Christ's disciples.

8. Dear brother bishops, through you I would like to reach out to all the priests of the United States, to thank them for the holiness of their lives and for their untiring zeal in helping the faithful to experience God's saving love. The joyful and responsible witness of your priests is an extraordinary tribute to the vitality of the Church in your dioceses. I invite you and them to renew each day your love for the priesthood and always to see in it the pearl of great price for which a man will sacrifice all else (cf. Mt 13:45). I pray especially for those who are experiencing difficulties in their vocation, and I entrust their worries and cares to the intercession of Mary, mother of the Redeemer.

As we celebrate today the feast of the ascension, we rejoice in the Lord's glory at the right hand of the Father, and we look towards the approaching feast of Pentecost. I invoke a fresh outpouring of the Holy Spirit upon you and upon the priests, religious, and laity of your dioceses. May the Paraclete who guides the Church in the task of evangelization renew his sevenfold gift in your hearts, so that with total fidelity you may love and serve the particular churches entrusted to your care. With my apostolic blessing.

FROM THE VATICAN, MAY 21, 1998

Joannes Paulus II

GREETING
OF THE BISHOPS
Region VII

Holy Father:

W^e are the bishops of three provinces from the midwestern section of the United States: the ecclesiastical provinces of Indianapolis, of Chicago, and of Milwaukee. We are grateful to be with you between the recent celebration of your birthday and the anticipated twentieth anniversary of your service to the universal Church as successor of Peter. We are grateful to be here during the week when the Church prays for the coming of the Holy Spirit at Pentecost and during the year of the Holy Spirit in preparation for the Great Jubilee.

In our local churches, this is the season of confirmation and ordination. The outpouring of the Holy Spirit upon those who are confirmed and those who are ordained priests is a source of hope for us. In the sacrament of confirmation, the Holy Spirit renews the faith, first given at baptism, of the young people given to our pastoral care. In the sacrament of holy orders, the Holy Spirit renews the pastoral care of the faithful with each newly ordained priest.

These signs of hope, these signs of the Holy Spirit's action shaping God's people, calm our occasional anxieties about ourselves and our ministry and bring us to you, so that you, guided by the Holy Spirit, can confirm the faith of your brother bishops from all parts of the American continent. Our U.S. conference will begin to discuss our own implementation of the Synod for America during our spring meeting next month. Already, a certain renewing of the bonds of unity among all the churches of America is happening as a result of your pastoral visit to Cuba, for which we are grateful. Those bonds will be further strengthened next January by your pilgrimage to Tepeyac in Mexico and to St. Louis, Mo., which borders our region.

With you now, we pray that the Great Jubilee will be a springtime for the Gospel. With you, at the threshold of the third millennium of Christianity, we see the mission of the Church being at the service of Christ's call to conversion of heart and mind, so that the world may be transformed. With you, we hope that the unity Christ desires all his disciples to enjoy may soon find again its roots in Sinai and Jerusalem and its full expression in the Apostolic See of Rome.

May the Virgin Mary, who gave birth to God's only begotten Son two thousand years ago by the power of the Holy Spirit, continue to give birth to Christ by her spiritual motherhood of his body, the Church, and may she guide and protect you and us so that Christ's leadership of the Church may become more clearly visible in our ministry.

CARDINAL FRANCIS E. GEORGE
ARCHBISHOP OF CHICAGO

ADDRESS OF POPE JOHN PAUL II

Region VII

Dear Cardinal George,
Dear Brother Bishops:

1. In the course of this series of *Ad Limina* visits, the bishops of the United States have again borne witness to the keen sense of communion of American Catholics with the successor of Peter. From the beginning of my pontificate, I have experienced this closeness and the spiritual and material support of so many of your people.

In welcoming you, the bishops of the ecclesiastical regions of Chicago, Indianapolis, and Milwaukee, I express once more to you and to the whole Church in your country my heartfelt gratitude: "God is my witness, whom I serve with my spirit in the gospel of his Son, that without ceasing I mention you always in my prayers" (Rom 1:9 [RSV]). Continuing the reflection begun with previous groups of bishops on the renewal of ecclesial life in the light of the Second Vatican Council and in view of the challenge of evangelization which we face on the eve of the next millennium, today I wish to address some aspects of your responsibility for Catholic education.

2. From the earliest days of the American republic, when Archbishop John Carroll encouraged the teaching vocation of St. Elizabeth Ann Seton and founded the new nation's first Catholic college, the Church in the United States has been deeply involved in edu-

cation at every level. For more than two hundred years, Catholic elementary schools, high schools, colleges, and universities have been instrumental in educating successive generations of Catholics and in teaching the truths of the faith, promoting respect for the human person and developing the moral character of their students. Their academic excellence and success in preparing young people for life have served the whole of American society.

As we approach the third Christian millennium, the Second Vatican Council's call for generous dedication to the whole enterprise of Catholic education remains to be more fully implemented (cf. *Gravissimum Educationis*, no. 1). Few areas of Catholic life in the United States need the leadership of the bishops for their reaffirmation and renewal as much as this one does. Any such renewal requires a clear vision of the Church's educational mission, which in turn cannot be separated from the Lord's mandate to preach the Gospel to all nations.

Like other educational institutions, Catholic schools transmit knowledge and promote the human development of their students. However, as the council emphasized, the Catholic school does something else: "It aims to create for the school community an atmosphere enlivened by the Gospel spirit of freedom and charity. It aims to help the young person in such a way that the development of his or her own personality will be matched by the growth of that new creation which he or she has become by baptism. It strives to relate all human culture eventually to the news of salvation, so that the light of faith will illumine the knowledge which students gradually gain of the world, of life, and of the human family" (ibid., no. 8). The mission of the Catholic school is the integral formation of students, so that they may be true to their condition as Christ's disciples and as such work effectively for the evangelization of culture and for the common good of society.

3. Catholic education aims not only to communicate facts but also to transmit a coherent, comprehensive vision of life, in the conviction

that the truths contained in that vision liberate students in the most profound meaning of human freedom. In its recent document *The Catholic School on the Threshold of the Third Millennium*, the Congregation for Catholic Education drew attention to the importance of communicating knowledge in the context of the Christian vision of the world, of life, of culture, and of history: "In the Catholic school there is no separation between time for learning and time for formation, between acquiring notions and growing in wisdom. The various school subjects do not present only knowledge to be attained but also values to be acquired and truths to be discovered" (no. 14).

The greatest challenge to Catholic education in the United States today, and the greatest contribution that authentically Catholic education can make to American culture, is to restore to that culture the conviction that human beings can grasp the truth of things, and in grasping that truth can know their duties to God, to themselves, and to their neighbors.

In meeting that challenge, the Catholic educator will hear an echo of Christ's words: "If you continue in my word, you are truly my disciples; and you will know the truth, and the truth will make you free" (Jn 8:31-32 [NRSV]). The contemporary world urgently needs the service of educational institutions which uphold and teach that truth is "that fundamental value without which freedom, justice and human dignity are extinguished" (*Veritatis Splendor*, no. 4).

To educate in the truth, and for genuine freedom and evangelical love, is at the very heart of the Church's mission. In a cultural climate in which moral norms are often thought to be matters of personal preference, Catholic schools have a crucial role to play in leading the younger generation to realize that freedom consists above all in being able to respond to the demands of the truth (cf. *Veritatis Splendor*, no. 84). The respect which Catholic elementary and secondary schools enjoy suggests that their commitment to transmitting moral wisdom is meeting a widely felt cultural need in your country. The example of bishops and pastors who, with the support of Catholic parents, have persevered in leadership in this field should encourage everyone's efforts to foster new dedication and new growth. The fact that some dioceses are involved in a program of school building is a significant sign of vitality and a great hope for the future.

4. Almost twenty-five years have passed since your conference issued *To Teach as Jesus Did*, a document which is still very relevant today. It emphasized the importance of another aspect of Catholic education: "More than any other program of education sponsored by the Church, the Catholic school has the opportunity and obligation to be . . . oriented to Christian service because it helps students acquire skills, virtues, and habits of heart and mind required for effective service to others" (no. 106).

On the basis of what they see and hear, students should become ever more aware of the dignity of every human person and gradually absorb the key elements of the Church's social doctrine and her concern for the poor. Catholic institutions should continue their tradition of commitment to the education of the poor in spite of the financial burdens involved. In some cases, it may be necessary to find ways to share the burden more evenly, so that parishes with schools are not left to shoulder it alone.

A Catholic school is a place where students live a shared experience of faith in God and where they learn the riches of Catholic culture. Taking proper account of the stages of human development, the freedom of individuals, and the rights of parents in the education of their children, Catholic schools must help students to deepen their personal relationship with God and to discover that all things human have their deepest meaning in the person and teaching of Jesus Christ.

Prayer and the liturgy, especially the sacraments of the eucharist and penance, should mark the rhythm of a Catholic school's life. Transmitting knowledge about the faith, though essential, is not sufficient. If students in Catholic schools are to gain a genuine experience of the Church, the example of teachers and others responsible for their formation is crucial: The witness of adults in the school community is a vital part of the school's identity.

Numberless religious and lay teachers and other personnel in Catholic schools down the years have shown how their professional competence and commitment are grounded in the spiritual, intellectual, and moral values of the Catholic tradition. The Catholic community in the United States and the whole country have been immeasurably blessed through the work of so many dedicated religious in schools in every part of your country.

I also know how much you value the dedication of the many lay men and women who, sometimes at great financial sacrifice, are involved in Catholic education because they believe in the mission of Catholic schools. If in some cases there has been an eroding of confidence in the teaching vocation, you must do all you can to restore that trust.

5. Catechesis, either in schools or in parish-based programs, plays a fundamental role in transmitting the faith. The bishop should encourage catechists to see their work as a vocation: as a privileged sharing in the mission of handing on the faith and accounting for the hope that is in us (cf. 1 Pt 3:15). The gospel message is the definitive response to the deepest longings of the human heart. Young Catholics have a right to hear the full content of that message in order to come to know Christ, the one who has overcome death and opened the way to salvation. Efforts to renew catechesis must be based on the premise that Christ's teaching, as transmitted in the Church and as authentically interpreted by the magisterium, has to be presented in all its richness, and the methodologies used have to respond to the nature of the faith as truth received (cf. 1 Cor 15:1). The work you have begun through your conference to evaluate catechetical texts by the standard of the *Catechism*

of the Catholic Church will help to ensure the unity and completeness of the faith as it is presented in your dioceses.

6. The Church's tradition of involvement in universities, which goes back almost a thousand years, quickly took root in the United States. Today Catholic colleges and universities can make an important contribution to the renewal of American higher education. To belong to a university community, as was my privilege during my days as a professor, is to stand at the crossroads of the cultures that have formed the modern world. It is to be a trustee of the wisdom of centuries and a promoter of the creativity that will transmit that wisdom to future generations.

At a time when knowledge is often thought to be fragmentary and never absolute, Catholic universities should be expected to uphold the objectivity and coherence of knowledge. Now that the centuries-old conflict between science and faith is fading, Catholic universities should be in the forefront of a new and long-overdue dialogue between the empirical sciences and the truths of faith.

If Catholic universities are to become leaders in the renewal of higher education, they must first have a strong sense of their own Catholic identity. This identity is not established once and for all by an institution's origins, but comes from its living within the Church today and always, speaking from the heart of the Church (*Ex corde Ecclesiae*) to the contemporary world. The Catholic identity of a university should be evident in its curriculum, in its faculty, in student activities, and in the quality of its community life. This is no infringement upon the university's nature as a true center of learning, where the truth of the created order is fully respected, but also ultimately illuminated by the light of the new creation in Christ.

The Catholic identity of a university necessarily includes the university's relationship to the local church and its bishop. It is sometimes said that a university that acknowledges a responsibility to any community or authority outside the relevant academic professional associations has lost both its independence and its integrity. But this is to detach freedom from its object, which is truth. Catholic universities understand that there is no contradiction between the free and vigorous pursuit of the truth and a "recognition of and adherence to the teaching authority of the Church in matters of faith and morals" (*Ex Corde Ecclesiae*, no. 27).

7. In safeguarding the Catholic identity of Catholic institutions of higher education, bishops have a special responsibility in relation to the work of theologians. If, as the whole Catholic tradition testifies, theology is to be done in and for the Church, then the question of theology's relationship to the teaching authority of the Church is not extrinsic— something imposed from outside—but rather intrinsic to theology as an ecclesial science. Theology itself is accountable to those to whom Christ has given responsibility for overseeing the ecclesial community and its stability in the truth. As the discussion on these questions deepens in your country, it must be the bishops' aim to see that the terms used are genuinely ecclesial in character.

In addition, bishops should take a personal interest in the work of university chaplaincies, not only in Catholic institutions but also in other colleges and universities where Catholic students are present. Campus ministry offers a notable opportunity to be close to young people at a significant time in their lives: ". . . The university chapel is called to be a vital center for promoting the Christian renewal of culture, in respectful and frank dialogue, in a clear and well-grounded perspective (cf. 1 Pt 3:15), in a witness which is open to questioning and capable of convincing" (Address to the European Congress of University Chaplains, May 1, 1998, no. 4). Young adults need the service of committed chaplains who can help them, intellectually and spiritually, to attain their full maturity in Christ.

8. Dear brother bishops: On the threshold of a new century and a new millennium, the Church continues to proclaim the capacity of human beings to know the truth and to grow into genuine freedom through their acceptance of that truth. In this respect, the Church is the defender of the moral insight on which your country was founded. Your Catholic schools are widely recognized as models for the renewal of American elementary and secondary education. Your Catholic colleges and universities can be leaders in the renewal of American higher education.

At a time when the relationship between freedom and moral truth is being debated on a host of issues at every level of society and government, Catholic scholars have the resources to contribute to an intellectual and moral renewal of American culture. As you work to strengthen Catholic education, and as you promote Catholic intellectual life in all its dimensions, may you enjoy the protection of the Blessed Virgin Mary, seat of wisdom. On the eve of the feast of Pentecost, I join you in invoking the gifts of the Holy Spirit upon the Church in the United States. With affection in the Lord, I cordially impart my apostolic blessing to you and to the priests, religious, and laity of your dioceses.

FROM THE VATICAN, MAY 30, 1998

Joannes Paulus II

GREETING
OF THE BISHOPS
Region VIII

Holy Father:

We the bishops of the provinces of Minnesota, North and South Dakota, representing ten dioceses and over 1.5 million Catholics, come to this *Ad Limina* visit with tremendous joy and anticipation. Thank you, Holy Father, for providing us with this chance to meet with you and the various dicasteries regarding the health of our respective dioceses. It is truly our privilege to do the work of the Church in our province. We pledge to you our love and obedience in union with the bishops of the world.

We are especially privileged to make our *Ad Limina* visit so near to the historic celebration of the Great Jubilee of the Year 2000. In your exhortation *Tertio Millennio Adveniente*, you stated that Mother Church will celebrate both Christ's birth two thousand years ago and the fact that Christ's Church has endured for two thousand years. Like the mustard seed in the Gospel, the Church has grown and become a great tree, able to cover the whole of humanity with her branches.

Although we represent one tiny branch of that tree, together we have worked diligently to continue the work which began nearly two thousand years ago to spread the Gospel to those assigned to our care. Similarly, we have made great progress as a province in not only caring for those of our own flock, but also in contributing to society through various initiatives designed to change the very social fabric of our communities. Our hope and prayer is that when our work is done, the name and face of Jesus Christ will remain as an indelible mark in every facet of society and in the hearts of every person with whom we have touched.

The preparation that went into the quinquennial reports which we have submitted and will discuss with you and the members of your staff has provided us a wonderful opportunity to assess both our strengths and areas of needed growth. However, words on paper can never adequately describe the sacrifice and dedication of the many individuals, both ordained and lay, who form the human pillars which bear the burden of such a tremendous challenge.

On behalf of all those whom we represent and serve, we promise you our prayers for good health that you might continue to carry out Christ's mission of love for this world for many years to come.

MOST REV. HARRY J. FLYNN
ARCHBISHOP OF ST. PAUL-MINNEAPOLIS

ADDRESS OF
POPE JOHN PAUL II
Region VIII

Dear Brother Bishops:

1. With great joy in the Lord I welcome you, the pastors of the Church in the states of Minnesota, North Dakota, and South Dakota, on your *Ad Limina* visit. The theme of my reflections with the bishops of your country this year is the duty, in view of the approaching new millennium, of renewed evangelization, for which the Second Vatican Council marvelously prepared the way. Today I wish to reflect on the laity in the Church's life and mission. The new evangelization that can make the twenty-first century a springtime of the Gospel is a task for the entire people of God, but will depend in a decisive way on the lay faithful being fully aware of their baptismal vocation and their responsibility for bringing the good news of Jesus Christ to their culture and society.

The fathers of the Second Vatican Council gave special attention to the dignity and mission of the lay faithful, urging them "in the Lord's name to give a glad, generous and prompt response to the impulse of the Holy Spirit and to the voice of Christ, who is giving them an especially urgent invitation at this moment" (*Apostolicam Actuositatem*, no. 33). In order to restore the needed balance to ecclesial life, the council dedicated an extremely rich chapter in *Lumen Gentium* to the role of the laity in the Church's saving mission, and it further developed this theme in the *Decree on the Apostolate of the Laity* (*Apostolicam Actuositatem*).

With specific reference to contemporary circumstances, that mission was specified still more concretely in the *Pastoral Constitution on the Church in the Modern World* (*Gaudium et Spes*). In these documents and others, the council sought to extend the great flourishing of the lay apostolate which had characterized previous decades. More and more lay people had taken to heart the stirring words of Pope Pius XII: "Lay believers are in the front line of church life; for them the Church is the animating principle of human society. Therefore, they in particular ought to have an ever clearer consciousness not only of belonging to the Church, but of being the Church" (Discourse, February 20, 1946).

2. It was in this context of vigorous lay action that the council could clearly affirm: "It is evident to everyone that all the faithful of Christ of whatever rank or status are called to the fullness of the Christian life and to the perfection of charity" (*Lumen Gentium*, no. 40); and the council's *Decree on the Apostolate of the Laity* makes it clear that lay people are called to exercise the apostolate in the Church and in the world (cf. *Apostolicam Actuositatem*, no. 5). Lay men and women have indeed responded to this call. Everywhere there has been a blossoming of various forms of lay participation in the Church's life and mission.

Much has also been done since the council to explore more deeply the theological basis for the vocation and mission of the laity. This development reached a certain maturity in the 1987 Synod of Bishops on the role of the laity, with the subsequent post-synodal apostolic exhortation *Christifideles Laici*, published on December 30, 1988. The synod indicated the concrete ways in which the council's rich teaching on the lay state could be further translated into practice. One of its principal achievements was to set the various ministries and charisms within the framework of an ecclesiology of communion (cf. *Christifideles Laici*, no. 21).

Thus it dealt with the specific role of the laity, not as an extension or derivation of the clerical and hierarchical role, but in relation to the fundamental truth that all the baptized receive the same sanctifying grace, the grace of justification by which each one becomes a "new creature," an adopted child of God, a "partaker of the divine nature," a member of Christ and co-heir with him, a temple of the Holy Spirit (cf. *Catechism of the Catholic Church*, no. 1265). All the faithful—both ordained ministers and laity—together form the one body of the Lord: "Here there cannot be Greek and Jew, circumcised and uncircumcised, barbarian, Scythian, slave, free man, but Christ is all, and in all" (Col 3:11 [RSV]).

We are witnessing a return to the authentic theology of the laity found in the New Testament, where the Church, the body of Christ, is the whole of the chosen race, the royal priesthood, the holy nation, God's own people (cf. 1 Pt 2:9), and not a portion of it. St. Paul reminds us that the growth of the body depends on every member playing its part: "If we live by the truth and in love, we shall grow completely into Christ, who is the head by whom the whole Body is fitted and joined together, every joint adding its own strength, for each individual part to work according to its function. So the body grows until it has built itself up in love" (Eph 4:15-16 [NJB]). In preparing for the great ecclesial event that was the Second Vatican Council, Pope John XXIII was so struck by these words that he declared that they deserved to be inscribed on the council's doors (cf. Address on Pentecost Sunday, June 5, 1960).

In an ecclesiology of communion, the Church's hierarchical structure is not a matter of power but of service, completely ordered to the holiness of Christ's members. The threefold duty to teach, sanctify, and govern, entrusted to Peter and the apostles and their successors, "has no other purpose except to form the Church in line with the ideal of sanctity already programmed and prefigured in Mary" (Address to the Roman Curia, December 22, 1987, no. 3).

The Marian dimension of the Church is prior to the Petrine or hierarchical dimension, "as well as being supreme and pre-eminent, richer in personal and communitarian implications for the various ecclesial vocations" (ibid.). If I mention these well-known truths, it is because everywhere in the Church, and not least in your country, we see the spread of a fresh and invigorating lay spirituality and the magnificent fruits of the laity's greater involvement in the Church's life.

As we approach the third Christian millennium, it is of paramount importance that the pope and the bishops, fully conscious of their own special ministry of service in the mystical body of Christ, continue to "stir and promote a deeper awareness among all the faithful of the gift and responsibility they share, both in association and as individuals, in the communion and mission of the Church" (*Christifideles Laici*, no. 2).

3. The liturgical renewal which the council ardently desired and fostered has resulted in the more frequent and lively participation of the lay faithful in the tasks proper to them in the liturgical assembly. Full, active, and conscious participation in the liturgy should give birth to a more vigorous lay witness in the world, not a confusion of roles in the worshiping community.

Based on the will of Christ himself, there is a fundamental distinction between the ordained ministry arising from the sacrament of holy orders and the functions open to lay people and founded on the sacraments of baptism, confirmation, and, for most, matrimony. The intention of the Holy See's recent *Instruction on Certain Questions Regarding the Collaboration of the Non-Ordained Faithful in the Sacred Ministry of Priests* has been to reaffirm and clarify the canonical and disciplinary norms regulating this area, by putting the relevant directives in relation to the theological and ecclesiological principles involved.

I urge you to ensure that the liturgical life of your communities is led and governed by the grace of Christ working through the Church, which the Lord intended as a hierarchical communion. The distinction between the priesthood of the faithful and the ministerial priesthood must always be respected, since it belongs to "the constitutive form which [Christ] indelibly impressed on his Church" (Discourse at the

Symposium on the Participation of the Lay Faithful in the Priestly Ministry, May 11, 1994, no. 3).

4. As the fathers at the 1987 Synod on the Laity pointed out, it is an inadequate understanding of the role of the laity which leads lay men and women to become so strongly interested in church services and tasks that they fail to become actively involved in their responsibilities in the professional, social, cultural, and political field (cf. *Christifideles Laici*, no. 2). The first requirement of the new evangelization is the actual witness of Christians who live by the Gospel: "Let your light shine before others, so that they may see your good works and give glory to your Father in heaven" (Mt 5:16 [NRSV]).

Since lay people are at the forefront of the Church's mission to evangelize all areas of human activity—including the workplace, the worlds of science and medicine, the world of politics, and the diverse world of culture—they must be strong enough and sufficiently catechized "to testify how the Christian faith constitutes the only valid response . . . to the problems and hopes that life poses to every person and society" (*Christifideles Laici*, no. 34).

As my predecessor Pope Paul VI put it: "Take a Christian or a handful of Christians who in the midst of their own community show their capacity for understanding and acceptance, their sharing of life and destiny with other people, their solidarity with the efforts of all for whatever is noble and good. Let us suppose that, in addition, they radiate in an altogether simple and unaffected way their faith in values that go beyond current values, and their hope in something that is not seen and that one would not dare to imagine. Through this wordless witness these Christians stir up irresistible questions in the hearts of those who see how they live: Why are they like this? Why do they live in this way? What or who is it that inspires them? Why are they in our midst? Such a witness is already a silent proclamation of the Good News and a very powerful and effective one" (*Evangelii Nuntiandi*, no. 21).

Through God's grace, your particular churches are all gifted with Catholic men and women eager to live a full Christian life and to work for Christ's kingdom in the world around them. The bishops must not fail them by a lack of pastoral leadership. In your ministry and governance you have to impress on everyone the importance of formation and adult catechesis, prayer and sacramental practice, a real commitment to the evangelization of culture, and the application of Christian moral and social doctrine in public and private life.

5. The immediate and in many ways most important arena of the laity's Christian witness is marriage and the family. Where family life is strong and healthy, the sense of community and solidarity is also strong, and this helps to build that "civilization of life and love" which must be everyone's aim. But where the family is weak, all human relationships are exposed to instability and fragmentation. Today the family is under pressure from many quarters: "The family is placed at the center of the great struggle between good and evil, between life and death, between love and all that is opposed to love. To the family is entrusted the task of striving, first and foremost, to unleash the forces of good, the source of which is found in Christ the redeemer of man" (cf. *Letter to Families*, no. 23). At a time when the very definitions of marriage and family are endangered by attempts to enshrine in legislation alternative and distorted notions of these basic human communities, your ministry must include the clear proclamation of the truth of God's original design. Since the Christian family is the "domestic church," couples must be helped to relate their family life in concrete ways to the life and mission of the Church (cf. *Familiaris Consortio*, no. 49). The parish should be a "family of families," helping in every way possible to nourish the spiritual life of parents and children through prayer, the word of God, the sacraments, and the witness of holiness and charity. Bishops and priests should be eager to help and encourage families in every way, and should give their support to groups and associations which promote family life.

67

While it is important that the local church respond to the needs of people in problem situations, pastoral planning should also give adequate attention to the needs of ordinary families seeking to live up to their vocation. These families are the backbone of society and the hope of the Church: the principal promoters of Christian family life are couples and families themselves, who have a special responsibility to be servants of other couples and families.

6. This year marks the thirtieth anniversary of the publication by my predecessor Pope Paul VI of the encyclical letter *Humanae Vitae*. The truth about human sexuality, and the Church's teaching on the sanctity of human life and on responsible parenthood, must be presented in the light of the theological development which has followed that document and in the light of the experience of couples who have faithfully followed this teaching. Many couples have experienced how natural family planning promotes mutual respect, encourages tenderness between husband and wife, and helps develop an authentic inner freedom (cf. *Catechism of the Catholic Church*, no. 2370; *Humanae Vitae*, no. 21).

Their experience deserves to be shared, for it is the living confirmation of the truth which *Humanae Vitae* teaches. In contrast, there is a growing awareness of the serious harm caused to marital relationships by recourse to artificial contraception, which, because it inevitably thwarts the total self-giving implied in the conjugal act, at one and the same time destroys its procreative meaning and weakens its unitive significance (cf. *Evangelium Vitae*, no. 13).

With courage and compassion, bishops, priests, and lay Catholics must seize the opportunity to propose to the sons and daughters of the Church, and to the whole of society, the truth about the special gift that is human sexuality. The false promises of the "sexual revolution" are now painfully obvious in the human suffering caused by unprecedented rates of divorce, by the scourge of abortion and its lasting effects on those involved. Yet the teaching of the magisterium, the development of the "theology of the body," and the experience of faithful Catholic couples have given Catholics in the United States a uniquely powerful and compelling opportunity to bring the truth about human sexuality into a society that sorely needs to hear it.

7. The multicultural reality of American society is a source of enrichment for the Church, but it also presents challenges to pastoral action. Many dioceses, because of past and continuing immigration, have a strong Hispanic presence. The Hispanic faithful bring their own particular gifts to the local church, not least the vitality of their faith and their deep sense of family values.

They also face enormous difficulties, and you are making great efforts to have priests and others appropriately trained to provide good pastoral care and needed services to minority families and communities. In the face of extremely active proselytism by other religious groups, instruction in the faith, the building up of living communities, attention to the needs of families and young people, the fostering of personal and family prayer, a spiritual and liturgical life centered on the eucharist, and genuine Marian devotion are all essential (cf. Address to Hispanics at Our Lady of Guadalupe Plaza, San Antonio, September 13, 1987). The Hispanic faithful should be able to feel that their natural place, their spiritual home, is in the heart of the Catholic community.

The same should be said about the members of the African American community, who also are a vital presence in all your churches. Their love for the word of God is a special blessing to be treasured. While the United States has made great progress in ridding itself of racial prejudice, continuous efforts are needed to ensure that Black Catholics are fully involved in the Church's life.

In your dioceses, as in other parts of the United States, there are not a few Native Americans, proud descendants of the original peoples of your land. I encourage your efforts to provide for their spiritual care, to support them as they strive to preserve the good and noble traditions of their culture, and to be close to them as they struggle to overcome the negative effects of the marginalization from which they have suffered for so long. In the one Church of Christ, every culture and race finds its home.

8. Finally, I wish to tell you of the great joy which I experienced last weekend in St. Peter's Square at the meeting of so many lay members of the various ecclesial movements and communities which represent a providential gift of the Holy Spirit to the Church of our time. These movements and communities share a strong commitment to the spiritual life and to missionary outreach. As instruments of conversion and authentic gospel witness, they render a magnificent service in helping the Church's members to respond to the universal call to holiness and to their vocation to transform worldly realities in the light of the gospel values of life, freedom, and love. They represent a genuine source of renewal and evangelization, and should therefore have an important place in your discernment and pastoral planning.

An extraordinary and surprising new springtime for the Church will blossom from the dynamic faith, living hope, and active charity of the lay men and women who open their hearts to the lifegiving presence of the Holy Spirit. As bishops our task is to teach, sanctify, and govern in the name of Christ, seeking always to bring to fruition the gifts and talents of the faithful entrusted to our care.

I urge you to encourage everyone to take their proper place in the Church and to become ever more personally responsible for her mission. Devote special attention to strengthening family life, as the essential condition of the well-being of individuals and society. Draw on the spiritual resources of the various cultures present in the Church in the United States, and direct them to the genuine renewal of the whole people of God.

Entrusting your episcopal ministry to the intercession of Mary, Help of Christians, I pray for the priests, religious, and lay faithful of your dioceses and I cordially impart my apostolic blessing.

FROM THE VATICAN, JUNE 6, 1998

Joannes Paulus II

GREETING
OF THE BISHOPS
Region IX

Most Holy Father:

It is a great honor for me to address you in the name of all your brother bishops present here today. We come from mid-America, from the four ecclesiastical provinces of Dubuque, Kansas City, Omaha, and St. Louis, which embrace the states of Iowa, Kansas, Nebraska, and Missouri.

We have come to Rome to venerate the tombs and to evoke in prayer the memory of the holy apostles Peter and Paul. Like Paul himself, we come here in order "to see Peter." For us this means to be confirmed in our faith by you, Holy Father, successor of Peter in the See of Rome.

We are deeply grateful to the Second Vatican Council for having confirmed for each of us who are ordinaries the honored title of being "vicar of Christ" in our dioceses, but the same council reserves to the bishop of Rome alone the title vicar of Christ, for the universal Church.

And so we acknowledge in your sacred person the special presence of Christ the good shepherd, the universal pastor of the Church. With us we bring the hopes and aspirations, the joys and sorrows of the people of God whom we are called to serve. We express to you the communion of their love and assure you of their prayers. Their support for you is inspired by their faith in the mystery of the Church.

With immense joy we look forward, next January, after the solemn celebration of the promulgation of the Synod for America in Mexico, to the visit of Your Holiness to St. Louis. So many of our people throughout the whole region have expressed the hope of being able to see you for the first time. There is a great expectation as Catholics and non-Catholics alike await your arrival.

Meanwhile, Holy Father, we ask you for your words of encouragement, your message of hope, and your apostolic blessing. We assure you of our filial love in Christ Jesus.

MOST REV. JUSTIN F. RIGALI
ARCHBISHOP OF ST. LOUIS

ADDRESS OF
POPE JOHN PAUL II
Region IX

Dear Brother Bishops:

1. On the occasion of your *Ad Limina* visit, I warmly welcome you, the pastors of the Church in the ecclesiastical region of St. Louis, Omaha, Dubuque, and Kansas City. Through you I greet the priests, religious, and lay faithful of your dioceses: "Grace, mercy, and peace from God the Father and Christ Jesus our Lord" (1 Tm 1:2 [RSV]). Continuing the theme of these *Ad Limina* talks, today it is my intention to devote my remarks to the reality of the consecrated life in the churches over which you and your brother bishops preside in charity and pastoral service. These brief reflections aim neither to be a full presentation of the consecrated life nor to address all the practical questions which come up in your relations with religious. Rather, I wish to support you in your ministry as successors of the apostles, a ministry which extends also to the consecrated persons living and working in your dioceses.

In particular, I wish to express a special word of appreciation, gratitude, and encouragement to the women and men who, through the observance of the evangelical counsels, make visible in the Church the form that the incarnate Son of God took upon himself during his earthly life (cf. *Vita Consecrata*, no. 14). By their consecration and fraternal life, they bear witness to the new creation inaugurated by Christ and made possible in us through the power of the Holy Spirit. By their prayer and sacrifice, they sustain the Church's fidelity to her saving mission. By their solidarity with the poor, they imitate the compassion of Jesus himself and his love of justice. By their intellectual apostolates, they serve the proclamation of the Gospel in the heart of the world's cultures. By giving their lives to the hardest tasks, countless consecrated women and men in the United States and all over the world testify to the supremacy of God and the ultimate significance of Jesus Christ for human life. Many of them are involved in missionary work, especially in Latin America, Africa, and Asia, and in recent times some of them have borne the ultimate witness by shedding their blood for the Gospel's sake.

The witness of consecrated persons makes tangible in the midst of God's people the spirit of the beatitudes, the value of the great commandment of love of God and love of neighbor. In a word, consecrated persons are at the very heart of the mystery of the Church, the bride who responds to Christ's infinite love with her whole being. How could we bishops fail to praise God unceasingly and be filled with gratitude for such a gift to his Church!

2. The gift of consecrated life forms an integral part of the pastoral solicitude of the successor of Peter and of the bishops. The indivisibility of the bishops' pastoral ministry means that they have a specific responsibility for overseeing all charisms and callings, and this translates into specific duties regarding the consecrated life as it exists in each particular church (cf. *Mutuae Relationes*, no. 9). Religious institutes for their part ought to be eager to establish a cordial and effective cooperation with the bishops (cf. ibid., no. 13), who by divine institution have succeeded the apostles as shepherds of the Church, so that whoever hears them hears Christ (cf. Lk 10:16; *Lumen Gentium*, no. 20).

The new springtime which the Church confidently awaits must also be a time of renewal and even rebirth of the consecrated life! The seeds of renewal are already showing many promising results, and the new institutes of consecrated life now taking their place alongside the older ones bear witness to the abiding relevance and appeal of the total gift of self to the Lord according to the charisms of the founders and foundresses.

3. Over a considerable period, religious life in the United States has been characterized by change and adaptation, as called for by the Second Vatican Council and codified in canon law and other magisterial documents. This has not been an easy time, since a renewal of such complexity and far-reaching consequences, involving so many people, could not take place without much effort and strain. It has not always been easy to strike a proper balance between necessary change and fidelity to the spiritual and canonical experience which had become a stable and fruitful part of the Church's living tradition. All of this has sometimes resulted in suffering for individual religious and for whole communities, a suffering which in some cases has brought new insights and a new commitment but which in other cases has resulted in disenchantment and discouragement.

Ever since the beginning of my pontificate, I have tried to encourage the bishops to engage religious communities in a dialogue of faith and fidelity, with the aim of helping religious to live their ecclesial vocation to the full. Down the years I have many times discussed the state of religious life in your country with religious themselves, as well as with the bishops and others concerned. In all the initiatives undertaken in this regard, it has been my intention on the one hand to affirm the personal and collegial responsibility for religious life which belongs to the bishops as the ones primarily responsible for the Church's holiness, doctrine, and mission, and on the other to affirm the importance and value of the consecrated life, and the extraordinary merits of so many consecrated women and men in every kind of service, at the side of suffering humanity.

Today I wish to invite the United States bishops to continue to foster personal contacts with the religious actually living and working in the individual dioceses in order to encourage and challenge them. Generally speaking, your relations with religious are truly friendly and cooperative, and in many cases they play an important part in your pastoral plans and projects. It is a matter of confirming that relationship in its natural setting, the context of dynamic communion with the local church.

The mission of religious places them in a definite particular church: their vocation to serve the universal Church, then, is exercised within the structures of the particular church (cf. Address to Superiors General, November 24, 1978). This is an important point, for many errors of judgment can result when a sound ecclesiology gives way to a concept of the Church too marked by civil and political terms, or so "spiritualized" that the individual's subjective choices become the criteria of behavior.

4. As bishops you have a duty to safeguard and proclaim the values of religious life, in order that they may be faithfully preserved and passed on within the life of your diocesan communities. Poverty and self-possession, consecrated chastity and fruitfulness, obedience and freedom: these paradoxes proper to the consecrated life need to be better understood and more fully appreciated by the whole Church, and in particular by those who have a part in educating the faithful. The theology and spirituality of the consecrated life need to be a part of the training of diocesan priests, just as attention to the theology of the particular church and to the spirituality of the diocesan clergy should be included in the formation of consecrated persons (cf. *Vita Consecrata*, no. 50).

In your contacts with religious, you will point to the importance of their community witness and show your willingness to help in whatever way possible to ensure that communities have the spiritual and material means to live the common life serenely and joyfully (cf. Congregation for Institutes of Consecrated Life and Societies of Apostolic Life, Fraternal Life in Community, February 2, 1994). One of the most valuable services that a bishop can provide is to ensure that good and experienced spiritual guides and confessors are available to religious, especially to monasteries of contemplative nuns and motherhouses with many members. Likewise, an institute's capacity to conduct a common or community apostolate is of vital concern to the life of a particular church. It is not enough that all members of an institute subscribe to the same general values, or work "according to the founding spirit," with each one responsible for finding some place of apostolic activity and a residence.

Obviously not every member of an institute will be suited to work in only one apostolate, but the identity and nature of the common apostolate, and the willingness to engage in it, should be an essential part of an institute's discerning of the vocation of its candidates. Only when a diocese can rely on a religious institute's commitment to a community apostolate can it engage seriously in long-range pastoral planning. Where institutes are already engaged in community apostolates such as education and health care, they should be encouraged and helped to persevere. Sensitivity to new needs and to the new poor, however necessary and laudable, should not entail neglect of the old poor, those in need of genuine Catholic education, the sick, and the elderly.

You should also encourage religious to give explicit attention to the specifically Catholic dimension of their activities. Only on this basis will Catholic schools and centers of higher learning be able to promote a culture imbued with Catholic values and morality; only in this way will Catholic health care facilities ensure that the sick and needy are taken care of "for the sake of Christ" and according to Catholic moral and ethical principles.

5. In many dioceses consecrated life is facing the challenge of declining numbers and advancing age. The bishops of the United States have already shown their readiness to lend assistance, and the Catholic faithful have demonstrated great generosity in providing financial support for religious institutes with particular needs in this area. Religious

communities themselves need to reaffirm their confidence in their calling and, relying on the help of the Holy Spirit, re-propose the ideal of consecration and mission. A presentation of the evangelical counsels merely in terms of their usefulness and convenience for a particular form of service is not enough. It is only personal experience, through faith, of Christ and of the mystery of his kingdom at work in human history which can make the ideal come alive in the minds and hearts of those who may be called.

At the approach of the new millennium, the Church urgently needs a vital and appealing religious life that shows forth concretely the sovereignty of God and bears witness before the world to the transcendent value of the "total gift of self in the profession of the evangelical counsels" (*Vita Consecrata*, no. 16), a gift which overflows in contemplation and service. This is surely the kind of challenge to which young people will respond. If it is true that the person becomes himself or herself through the sincere gift of self (cf. *Gaudium et Spes*, no. 24), then there should be no hesitation in calling the young to consecration. It is in fact a call to full human and Christian maturity and fulfillment.

Perhaps the Great Jubilee might be an occasion for institutes of consecrated life to set up and support new communities of their members who are seeking an authentic, stable, and community-centered experience according to the spirit of the founders and foundresses. In many cases this would permit religious to commit themselves more serenely to these goals, free from burdens and problems which ultimately cannot be resolved.

6. The two thousandth anniversary of the birth of the Savior invites the whole Church to be absorbed with bringing Christ to the world. She must proclaim his victory over sin and death, a victory brought about in his blood on the cross, and every day made truly present in the eucharist. We know that genuine hope for the future of the human family lies in presenting clearly to the world the incarnate Son of God as the

exemplar of all human life. Religious in particular should be ready to make this proclamation in openness to the sanctifying power of the Holy Spirit and with complete inner freedom from any residual fear of displeasing the "world," understood as a culture which promises a liberation and salvation different from those of Christ.

This is no vain triumphalism or presumption, for in every age Christ is "the power of God and the wisdom of God" (1 Cor 1:24 [RSV]). In our day, as throughout the history of the Church, consecrated women and men stand out as living icons of what it means to make the following of Jesus the whole purpose of one's life and to be transformed by his grace. In fact, as the apostolic exhortation *Vita Consecrata* points out: Religious "have set out on a journey of continual conversion, of exclusive dedication to the love of God and of [their] brothers and sisters, in order to bear ever more splendid witness to the grace which transfigures Christian life" (no. 109). Because Christ will never fail his Church, religious have "not only a glorious history to remember and to recount, but also a great history still to be accomplished!" (ibid., no. 110).

7. Dear brother bishops, through you I earnestly exhort the women and men religious who have borne the "burden of the day and the scorching heat" (Mt 20:12) to persevere in their faithful witness. There is a way of living the cross with bitterness and sadness, but it breaks our spirit. There is also the way of carrying the cross as Christ did, and then we perceive clearly that it leads "into glory" (cf. Lk 24:26). Through you, I appeal to all consecrated persons, and to the men and women who may be thinking of entering a community, to renew each day their awareness of the extraordinary privilege that is theirs: the call to serve the holiness of God's people, to "be holiness" in the heart of the Church.

With your leadership and guidance, the future of the consecrated life in your country will certainly be glorious and fruitful. May the Blessed Virgin Mary, who, since she belongs completely to God and is totally devoted to him, is the sublime example of perfect consecration, accompany the renewal and the new flourishing of the consecrated life in the United States. To you and to the priests, religious, and laity of your dioceses, I cordially impart my apostolic blessing.

From the Vatican, June 13, 1998

Joannes Paulus II

GREETING
OF THE BISHOPS

Region X

Your Holiness, John Paul II:

We, the archbishops, bishops, and auxiliary bishops of two metropolitan sees, San Antonio and Oklahoma, U.S.A., cordially and joyfully greet you and all the members of your staff. We congratulate Your Holiness on your recent birthday and anniversary of ordination.

You have outlived all your predecessors of this century as the longest ruling pope: Congratulations! In spite of your suffering, as a result of the violent attack against you, you have continued to be in contact with God's people by your visits to many countries and receiving visitors in the Vatican for many hours daily. You have had a profound concern in material and spiritual needs of all the people the world over. No one in our time has rendered greater service in society than you have and will continue to do so. We promise to give you all our support and to have you in our daily prayers.

Your message to us is very timely. You help us to realize that God's people will accept and live the word of God if we not only preach with words but practice what we preach. You do both well: You teach in great words, but you practice what you preach. For the end of this millennium, you are urging us all to strive for reconciliation. You remind us that we as Church have hurt or offended others. You have given us a heroic example by your apologizing to our Jewish brothers and sisters for what took place at the Holocaust. You have asked for forgiveness from all others who have been offended in any way by you and by all of us, the Church. This reconciliation effort is indeed a tremendous act of courage and love. By so doing, you have taught the whole world that peace is only so far away as we are willing to repent: ask for forgiveness and be willing to forgive.

We know, too, that we have a cross to bear. The cross implies different elements at different times in history. Presently, our pain flows from the problems we face: the declining number of priests and religious men and women. The increasing difficulties of our priests and other key personnel. The horrendous lawsuits we face in several dioceses. The bad publicity we receive on television and the printed press. The financial pressures we endure. Our American society is suffering profoundly because of the epidemic of drugs, alcohol, and AIDS. The great number of prisons which are being built is unbelievable, and this is just the beginning. We have now more penitentiaries than colleges and universities, more prisoners than students. Violence in the homes, violence in the school, even at elementary levels, violence in the streets, drive-by shootings: violence is so horrendous that we have become our own worst enemies. However, Your Holiness, we are a people of hope. Jesus the Redeemer has promised to be with us until the end of time. We are not alone. We will continue to work for justice. We will be ready to grant forgiveness; we will be able to beg for forgiveness.

MOST REV. PATRICK F. FLORES
ARCHBISHOP OF SAN ANTONIO

ADDRESS OF
POPE JOHN PAUL II

Region X

Dear Brother Bishops:

1. I warmly welcome you, the pastors of the Church in the states of Texas, Oklahoma, and Arkansas, on the occasion of your *Ad Limina* visit. In my meetings so far this year with the United States bishops, we have considered some principal aspects of the new evangelization called for by the Second Vatican Council, the great event of grace by which the Holy Spirit has prepared the Church to enter the third Christian millennium. One essential part of this task is the proclamation of moral truth and its application to the personal lives of Christians and to their involvement in the world. Therefore, I wish to reflect with you today on your episcopal ministry as teachers of moral truth and witnesses to the moral law.

In every age, men and women need to hear Christ the Good Shepherd calling them to faith and conversion of life (cf. Mk 1:15). As shepherds of souls, you must be Christ's voice today, encouraging your people to rediscover "the beauty of truth, the liberating force of God's love, and the value of unconditional fidelity to all the demands of the Lord's law, even in the most difficult situations" (*Veritatis Splendor*, no. 107). The question posed by the rich young man in the Gospel— "Teacher, what good deed must I do, to have eternal life?" (Mt 19:16 [RSV])—is a perennial human question. It is asked in one form or another, explicitly or implicitly, by every human being in every culture and at every moment in the drama of history. Christ's answer to that question—to follow him in doing the will of his Father—is the key to the fullness of life which he promises. Obedience to God's commandments, far from alienating us from our humanity, is the pathway to genuine liberation and the source of true happiness.

In this year of preparation for the great jubilee dedicated to the Holy Spirit, let us remember that our efforts to preach the good news and teach the moral truth about the human person are sustained by the Spirit, who is the principal agent in the Church's mission (cf. *Evangelium Nuntiandi*, no. 64). It is the Holy Spirit who "brings about the flourishing of Christian moral life and the witness of holiness amid the great variety of vocations, gifts, responsibilities, conditions and life situations" (*Veritatis Splendor*, no. 108). In your dioceses and parishes, I urge you to make a special effort this year to increase awareness of the powerful activity of the Spirit in the world, for it is through his grace that we experience a "radical personal and social renewal capable of ensuring justice, solidarity, honesty and openness" (ibid., no. 98).

2. Given the circumstances of contemporary culture, your episcopal ministry is especially challenging, and the situation which you face as teachers of moral truth is complex. Your parishes are filled with Catholics eager to lead responsible lives as spouses, parents, citizens, workers, and professionals. These men and women, whom you meet daily in the course of your pastoral mission, know that they should live morally upright lives, but often they find it difficult to explain exactly what this implies.

This difficulty reflects another side of contemporary culture: "the skepticism regarding the very existence of moral truth" and an objective moral law. This attitude is quite prevalent in the cultural institutions that influence public opinion, and, it must be said, is commonplace in many of your country's academic, political, and legal structures. In this situation, those who try to live according to the moral law often feel pressured by forces which contradict the things they know in their hearts to be true. And those responsible for teaching moral truth may feel as if their task is virtually impossible, given the power of those external cultural pressures.

There have been similar moments in the course of the Church's two thousand-year history. Yet today's cultural crisis has distinctive characteristics that give your task as moral teachers a real urgency. This urgency touches both the transmission of the moral truth contained in the Gospel and the magisterium of the Church, and the future of society as a free and democratic way of life.

How should we define this crisis of moral culture? We can glimpse its first phase in what Cardinal John Henry Newman wrote in his letter to the Duke of Norfolk: "In this century [conscience] has been superseded by a counterfeit, which the eighteen centuries prior to it never heard of, and could not have mistaken for it, if they had. It is the right of self-will." What was true in Newman's nineteenth century is even truer today. Culturally powerful forces insist that the rights of conscience are violated by the very idea that there exists a moral law inscribed in our humanity, which we can come to know by reflecting on our nature and our actions, and which lays certain obligations upon us because we recognize them as universally true and binding. This, it is frequently said, is an abrogation of freedom. But what is the concept of "freedom" at work here? Is freedom merely an assertion of my will—"I should be permitted to do this because I choose to do it"? Or is freedom the right to do what I ought to do, to adhere freely to what is good and true (cf. Homily at Baltimore, October 8, 1995)?

The notion of freedom as personal autonomy is superficially attractive; endorsed by intellectuals, the media, legislatures, and the courts, it becomes a powerful cultural force. Yet it ultimately destroys the personal good of individuals and the common good of society. Freedom-as-autonomy, by its singleminded focus on the autonomous will of the individual as the sole organizing principle of public life, dissolves the bonds of obligation between men and women, parents and children, the strong and the weak, majorities and minorities. The result is the break-down of civil society, and a public life in which the only actors of consequence are the autonomous individual and the state. This, as the twentieth century ought to have taught us, is a sure prescription for tyranny.

3. At its roots, the contemporary crisis of moral culture is a crisis of understanding of the nature of the human person. As pastors and teachers of the Church of Christ, you remind people that the greatness of human beings is founded precisely in their being creatures of a loving God, who gave them the capacity to know the good and to choose it, and who sent his Son to be the final and unsurpassable witness to the truth about the human condition: "In Christ and through Christ, God has revealed himself fully to mankind and has definitively drawn close to it; at the same time, in Christ and through Christ man has acquired full awareness of his dignity, of the heights to which he is raised, of the surpassing worth of his own humanity, and of the meaning of his existence" (*Redemptor Hominis*, no. 11). In Christ, we know that "the good of the person lies in being in the truth and doing the truth" (Address to the International Congress of Moral Theology, April 10, 1986, no. 1).

In this Christian anthropology, the nobility of men and women lies not simply in the capacity to choose, but in the capacity to choose wisely and to live according to that choice of what is good. In all of visible creation, only the human person chooses reflectively. Only the human person can discern between good and evil and give reasons justifying that discernment. Only human beings can make sacrifices for what is good and true. That is why, throughout Christian history, the martyr remains the paradigm of discipleship: for the martyr lives out the relationship between truth, freedom, and goodness in the most radical way.

By teaching the moral truth about the human person and witnessing to the moral law inscribed on the human heart, the bishops of the

Church are defending and promoting not arbitrary claims made by the Church but essential truths, and therefore the good of individuals and the common good of society.

4. If the dignity of the human person as a moral agent rests on the capacity to know and choose what is truly good, then the question of conscience comes into clearer focus. Respect for the rights of conscience is deeply ingrained in your national culture, which was formed in part by emigrants who came to the New World to vindicate their religious and moral convictions in the face of persecution. American society's historic admiration for men and women of conscience is the ground on which you can teach the truth about conscience today.

The Church honors conscience as the "sanctuary" of the human person: here, men and women are "alone with God," whose voice echoes in the depths of their hearts, summoning them to love good and avoid evil (cf. *Gaudium et Spes*, no. 16). Conscience is that inner place where "man detects a law which he does not impose upon himself, but which holds him to obedience" (ibid.). This being the case, the dignity of conscience is demeaned when it is suggested, as the defenders of radical individual autonomy claim, that conscience is a wholly independent, exclusively personal capacity to determine what constitutes good and evil (cf. *Dominum et Vivificantem*, no. 43).

Everyone must act in accordance with conscience. But conscience is neither absolutely independent nor infallible in its judgments; if it were, conscience would be reduced to the mere assertion of personal will. Thus it is precisely a defense of the dignity of conscience and of the human person to teach that consciences must be formed, so that they can discern what actually does or does not correspond to the "eternal, objective and universal divine law" which human intelligence is capable of discovering in the order of being (cf. *Dignitatis Humanae*, no. 3; *Veritatis Splendor*, no. 60). Because of the nature of conscience, the admonition always to follow it must immediately be followed by the question of whether what our conscience is telling us is true or not. If we fail to make this necessary clarification, conscience—instead of being that holy place where God reveals to us our true good—becomes a force which is destructive of our true humanity and of all our relationships (cf. General Audience, August 17, 1983, no. 3).

As bishops you have to teach that freedom of conscience is never freedom from the truth but always and only freedom in the truth. This understanding of conscience and its relationship to freedom should clarify certain aspects of the question of dissent from church teaching. By the will of Christ himself and the lifegiving power of the Holy Spirit, the Church is preserved in the truth and "it is her duty to give utterance to, and authoritatively to teach, that truth which is Christ himself, and to declare and confirm by her authority those principles of the moral order which have their origin in human nature itself' (*Dignitatis Humanae*, no. 14).

When the Church teaches, for example, that abortion, sterilization, or euthanasia are always morally inadmissible, she is giving expression to the universal moral law inscribed on the human heart and is therefore teaching something which is binding on everyone's conscience. Her absolute prohibition that such procedures be carried out in Catholic health care facilities is simply an act of fidelity to God's law. As bishops you must remind everyone involved—hospital administrations and medical personnel—that any failure to comply with this prohibition is both a grievous sin and a source of scandal (for sterilizations, cf. Congregation for the Doctrine of the Faith, *Quaecumque Sterilizatio*, March 13, 1975, *AAS* [1976]: 738-740). This and other such instances are not, it must be emphasized, the imposition of an external set of criteria in violation of human freedom. Rather, the Church's teaching of moral truth "brings to light the truths which [conscience] ought already to possess" (*Veritatis Splendor*, no. 64), and it is these truths which make us free in the deepest meaning of human freedom and give our humanity its genuine nobility.

Almost two thousand years ago, St. Paul urged us to "not be conformed to this world" but to live the true freedom that is obedience to the will of God (Rom 12:2). In teaching the truth about conscience and its intrinsic relationship to moral truth, you will be challenging one of the great forces in the modern world. But at the same time, you will be doing the modern world a great service, for you will be reminding it of the only foundation capable of sustaining a culture of freedom: what the founders of your nation called "self-evident" truths.

5. From this perspective, it should be clear that the Church addresses issues of public life not for political reasons but as a servant of the truth about the human person, a defender of human dignity and a promoter of human freedom. A society or culture which wishes to survive cannot declare the spiritual dimension of the human person to be irrelevant to public life. Cultures develop as ways of dealing with the most profound experiences of human existence: love, birth, friendship, work, death. Each of these experiences raises, in its unique way, the question of God: "at the heart of every culture lies the attitude man takes to the greatest mystery: the mystery of God" (*Centesimus Annus*, no. 24). American Catholics, in common with other Christians and all believers, have a responsibility to ensure that the mystery of God and the truth about humanity that is revealed in the mystery of God are not banished from public life.

This is especially important for democratic societies, since one of the truths contained in the mystery of our creation by God is that the human person must be "the origin, the subject and the purpose of all social institutions" (*Gaudium et Spes*, no. 25). Our intrinsic dignity and inalienable fundamental rights are not the result of social convention: They precede all social conventions and provide the norms that determine their validity. The history of the twentieth century is a grim warning of the evils that result when human beings are reduced to the status of objects to be manipulated by the powerful for selfish gain or for ideological reasons. In proclaiming the truth that God has given men and women an inestimable dignity and inalienable rights from the moment of conception, you are helping to rebuild the moral foundations of a genuine culture of freedom, capable of sustaining institutions of self-governance that serve the common good.

6. It is a tribute to the Church and to the openness of American society that so many Catholics in the United States are involved in political life. As pastors and teachers, your responsibility to Catholic public officials is to remind them of the heritage of reflection on the moral law, on society, on democracy, which they ought to bring to their office.

Your country prides itself on being a realized democracy, but democracy is itself a moral adventure, a continuing test of a people's capacity to govern themselves in ways that serve the common good and the good of individual citizens. The survival of a particular democracy depends not only on its institutions, but to an even greater extent on the spirit which inspires and permeates its procedures for legislating, administering, and judging. The future of democracy, in fact, depends on a culture capable of forming men and women who are prepared to defend certain truths and values. It is imperiled when politics and law are sundered from any connection to the moral law written on the human heart.

If there is no objective standard to help adjudicate between different conceptions of the personal and common good, then democratic politics is reduced to a raw contest for power. If constitutional and statutory law are not held accountable to the objective moral law, the first casualties are justice and equity, for they become matters of personal opinion. Catholics in public life render a particularly important service to society when they defend objective moral norms as "the unshakable foundation and solid guarantee of a just and peaceful human coexistence, and hence of genuine democracy," for it is through our common obligation to these moral norms that we come to know, and can defend, the equality of all citizens, "who possess common rights and duties" (*Veritatis Splendor*, no. 96).

A climate of moral relativism is incompatible with democracy. That kind of culture cannot answer questions fundamental to a democratic political community: "Why should I regard my fellow citizen as my equal?"; "Why should I defend someone else's rights?"; "Why should I work for the common good?" If moral truths cannot be publicly acknowledged as such, democracy is impossible (cf. *Veritatis Splendor*, no. 101). Thus I wish to encourage you to continue to speak out clearly and effectively about the fundamental moral questions facing people today. The interest with which many of your documents have been received throughout society is an indication that you are providing much-needed guidance when you remind everyone, and especially Catholic citizens and Catholic political leaders, of the essential bond between freedom and truth.

7. Dear brother bishops, a time of "crisis" is a time of opportunity as well as a time of danger. That is certainly true of the crisis of moral culture in the developed world today. The call of the Second Vatican Council to the people of God to witness to the truth about the human person amidst the joy and hope, grief and pain, of the contemporary world is a call to all of us for a personal commitment to effective episcopal leadership in the new evangelization. By focusing the attention of the faithful and all your fellow citizens on the extremely serious moral choices before them, you will help to bring about that renewal of moral goodness, solidarity, and genuine freedom which the United States and the world urgently need. Entrusting your ministry, and the priests, religious, and laity of your dioceses to the protection of Mary, patroness of the United States under the great

title of her Immaculate Conception, I cordially impart my apostolic blessing.

From the Vatican, June 27, 1998

Joannes Paulus II

GREETING
OF THE BISHOPS
Region XI

Most Holy Father:

The bishops of Region XI of the United States of America, representing the archdioceses and dioceses on the western coast of our country, express our collective gratitude to you for receiving us on our visit *Ad Limina Apostolorum.*

While all of the activities of our *Ad Limina* visit are important, none is more meaningful to us than to gather for the celebration of the holy eucharist celebrated by Your Holiness. The Second Vatican Council reminded us of the great power of the celebration of the eucharist and the sacramental life of the Church: "The liturgy is the summit toward which the activity of the church is directed; it is also the fount from which all her power flows."[1]

We come, Holy Father, to renew our bonds of collegiality with you, to be strengthened in our ministry, the important pastoral task Jesus urged upon Peter: "I have prayed that your own faith may not fail; . . . you must strengthen your brothers."[2] As we progress forward to crossing the threshold of the third millennium of Christ's redeeming mission upon earth, we eagerly follow your inspired and prophetic leadership, we embrace with enthusiasm your call to a new and fuller evangelization of the world and its cultures, and we labor within our local churches to build up the body of Christ in both integrity and charity.

Our local churches are experiencing a remarkable growth in new Catholics, primarily through the arrival of immigrants from throughout

Latin America, Asia, and the Pacific Islands. As a result, our parishes are laboring diligently to meet the spiritual and pastoral needs of many multiethnic groups. Our region of the United States has become the most diverse in the country, placing new pastoral challenges upon us, your collaborators in the mission of Jesus Christ. We look to you for both guidance and encouragement as we strive to meet these increasing needs.

Most Holy Father, we renew our filial bonds of fidelity to you, the successor of Peter and the vicar of Christ upon earth; we deepen those links between our particular churches and the church of Rome, thus enriching the collegiality that unites us all; and we surround you with our prayers and support as we draw ever closer to the new millennium, a new and fresh moment for the salvation of the world in and through Jesus Christ!

CARDINAL ROGER M. MAHONY
ARCHBISHOP OF LOS ANGELES

Notes

1.   *Sacrosanctum Concilium*, December 4, 1963, no. 10.
2.   Lk 22:32 [NAB].

ADDRESS OF
POPE JOHN PAUL II

Region XI

Dear Cardinal Mahony,
Dear Brother Bishops:

1. With joy and affection I welcome you, the bishops of the Church in California, Nevada, and Hawaii, on the occasion of your visit *Ad Limina Apostolorum*. Your pilgrimage to the tombs of the apostles Peter and Paul is a celebration of the ecclesial bonds linking your particular churches to the See of Peter. Mindful that the Church throughout the world is preparing to celebrate the Great Jubilee of the Year 2000, I have chosen to devote this series of reflections with you and your brother bishops to the renewal of the Church's life envisaged by the Second Vatican Council.

The council was a gift of the Holy Spirit to the Church, and its full implementation is the best means of ensuring that the Catholic community in the United States enters the new millennium strengthened in faith and holiness, effectively contributing to a better society through its witness to the truth about man that is revealed in Jesus Christ (cf. *Gaudium et Spes*, no. 24). Indeed, the marvelous responsibility of the Church in your country is to spread this truth, which "enlightens man's intelligence and shapes his freedom, leading him to know and love the Lord" (*Veritatis Splendor*, preamble).

We are coming to the end of a century which began with confidence in humanity's prospects of almost unlimited progress, but which is now ending in widespread fear and moral confusion. If we want a springtime of the human spirit, we must rediscover the foundations of hope (cf. Address to the 50th General Assembly of the United Nations, October 5, 1995, nos. 16-18). Above all, society must learn to embrace once more the great gift of life, to cherish it, to protect it, and to defend it against the culture of death, itself an expression of the great fear that stalks our times. One of your most noble tasks as bishops is to stand firmly on the side of life, encouraging those who defend it and building with them a genuine culture of life.

2. The Second Vatican Council was quite aware of the forces shaping contemporary society when it spoke out clearly in defense of human life against the many threats facing it (cf. *Gaudium et Spes*, no. 27). The council also made a priceless contribution to the culture of life by its eloquent presentation of the full meaning of married love (cf. ibid., nos. 48-51). Following the lead of the council and expounding its teaching, Pope Paul VI wrote the prophetic encyclical *Humanae Vitae*, the thirtieth anniversary of which we are celebrating this year, in which he addressed the moral implications of the power to cooperate with the Creator in bringing new life into the world. The Creator has made man and woman to complement one another in love, and their union is no less than a sharing in the creative power of God himself. Conjugal love serves life not only insofar as it generates new life but also because, rightly understood as the total gift of spouses to one another, it shapes the loving and caring context in which new life is wholeheartedly welcomed as a gift of incomparable value.

Thirty years after *Humanae Vitae*, we see that mistaken ideas about the individual's moral autonomy continue to inflict wounds on the consciences of many people and on the life of society. Paul VI pointed out some of the consequences of separating the unitive aspect of conjugal love from its procreative dimension: a gradual weakening of moral discipline; a trivialization of human sexuality; the demeaning of women; marital infidelity, often leading to broken families; state-sponsored programs of population control based on imposed contraception and sterilization (cf. *Humanae Vitae*, no. 17). The introduction of legalized abortion and euthanasia, ever increasing recourse to in vitro fertilization, and certain forms of genetic manipulation and embryo experimentation are also closely related in law and public policy, as well as in contemporary culture, to the idea of unlimited dominion over one's body and life.

The teaching of *Humanae Vitae* honors married love, promotes the dignity of women, and helps couples grow in understanding the truth of their particular path to holiness. It is also a response to contemporary culture's temptation to reduce life to a commodity. As bishops, together with your priests, deacons, seminarians, and other pastoral personnel, you must find the right language and imagery to present this teaching in a comprehensible and compelling way. Marriage preparation programs should include an honest and complete presentation of the Church's teaching on responsible procreation, and should explain the natural methods of regulating fertility, the legitimacy of which is based on respect for the human meaning of sexual intimacy. Couples who have embraced the teaching of Pope Paul VI have discovered that it is truly a source of profound unity and joy, nourished by their increased mutual understanding and respect; they should be invited to share their experience with engaged couples taking part in marriage preparation programs.

3. Reflection on a very different anniversary serves to heighten the sense of the urgency of the pro-life task. In the twenty-five years which have passed since the judicial decision legalizing abortion in your country there has been a widespread mobilization of consciences in support of life. The pro-life movement is one of the most positive aspects of American public life, and the support given it by the bishops is a tribute to your pastoral leadership. Despite the generous efforts of so many, however, the idea that elective abortion is a "right" continues to be

asserted. Moreover, there are signs of an almost unimaginable insensitivity to the reality of what actually happens during an abortion, as evidenced in recent events surrounding so-called "partial-birth" abortion. This is a cause for deep concern. A society with a diminished sense of the value of human life at its earliest stages has already opened the door to a culture of death. As pastors, you must make every effort to ensure that there is no dulling of consciences regarding the seriousness of the crime of abortion, a crime which cannot be morally justified by any circumstance, purpose, or law (cf. *Evangelium Vitae*, no. 62).

Those who would defend life must make alternatives to abortion increasingly visible and available. Your recent pastoral statement, *Lights and Shadows*, draws attention to the need to support women in crisis pregnancies and to provide counseling services for those who have had an abortion and must cope with its psychological and spiritual effects. Likewise, the unconditional defense of life must always include the message that true healing is possible, through reconciliation with the body of Christ. In the spirit of the coming Great Jubilee of the Year 2000, American Catholics should be more than ever willing to open their hearts and their homes to "unwanted" and abandoned children, to young people in difficulty, to the handicapped, and those who have no one to care for them.

4. The Church likewise offers a truly vital service to the nation when she awakens public awareness to the morally objectionable nature of campaigns for the legalization of physician-assisted suicide and euthanasia. Euthanasia and suicide are grave violations of God's law (cf. *Evangelium Vitae*, nos. 65 and 66); their legalization introduces a direct threat to the persons least capable of defending themselves, and it proves most harmful to the democratic institutions of society. The fact that Catholics have worked successfully with members of other Christian communities to resist efforts to legalize physician-assisted suicide is a very hopeful sign for the future of ecumenical public wit-

ness in your country, and I urge you to build an even broader ecumenical and interreligious movement in defense of the culture of life and the civilization of love.

As ecumenical witness in defense of life develops, a great teaching effort is needed to clarify the substantive moral difference between discontinuing medical procedures that may be burdensome, dangerous, or disproportionate to the expected outcome—what the *Catechism of the Catholic Church* calls "the refusal of 'overzealous' treatment" (no. 2278; cf. *Evangelium Vitae*, no. 65)—and taking away the ordinary means of preserving life, such as feeding, hydration, and normal medical care. The statement of the U.S. bishops' pro-life committee, *Nutrition and Hydration: Moral and Pastoral Considerations*, rightly emphasizes that the omission of nutrition and hydration intended to cause a patient's death must be rejected and that, while giving careful consideration to all the factors involved, the presumption should be in favor of providing medically assisted nutrition and hydration to all patients who need them. To blur this distinction is to introduce a source of countless injustices and much additional anguish, affecting both those already suffering from ill health or the deterioration which comes with age, and their loved ones.

5. In a culture that has difficulty in defining the meaning of life, death, and suffering, the Christian message is the good news of Christ's victory over death and the certain hope of resurrection. The Christian accepts death as the supreme act of obedience to the Father, and is ready to meet death at the "hour" known only to him (cf. Mk 13:32). Life is a pilgrimage in faith to the Father, on which we travel in the company of his Son and the saints in heaven.

Precisely for this reason, the very real trial of suffering can become a source of good. Through suffering, we actually have a part in Christ's redemptive work for the Church and humanity (cf. *Salvifici Doloris*, nos. 14-24). This is so when suffering is "experienced for love and with love through sharing, by God's gracious gift and one's own personal and free choice, in the suffering of Christ crucified" (*Evangelium Vitae*, no. 67).

The work of Catholic health care institutions in meeting the physical and spiritual needs of the sick is a form of imitation of Christ who, in the words of St. Ignatius of Antioch, is "the doctor of the flesh and of the spirit" (*Ad Ephesios*, 7, 2). Doctors, nurses, and other medical personnel deal with people in their time of trial, when they have an acute sense of life's fragility and precariousness—just when they most resemble the suffering Jesus in Gethsemane and on Calvary. Health care professionals should always bear in mind that their work is directed to individuals, unique persons in whom God's image is present in a singular way and in whom he has invested his infinite love. The sickness of a family member, friend, or neighbor is a call to Christians to demonstrate true compassion, that gentle and persevering sharing in another's pain. Likewise, the handicapped and those who are ill must never feel that they are a burden; they are persons being visited by the Lord. The terminally ill in particular deserve the solidarity, communion, and affection of those around them; they often need to be able to forgive and to be forgiven, to make peace with God and with others. All priests should appreciate the pastoral importance of celebrating the sacrament of the anointing of the sick, particularly when it is the prelude to the final journey to the Father's house: when its meaning as the *sacramentum exeuntium* is particularly evident (cf. *Catechism of the Catholic Church*, no. 1523).

6. An essential feature of support for the inalienable right to life, from conception to natural death, is the effort to provide legal protection for the unborn, the handicapped, the elderly, and those suffering from terminal illness. As bishops, you must continue to draw attention to the relationship of the moral law to constitutional and positive law in your society: "Laws which legitimize the direct killing of innocent

human beings . . . are in complete opposition to the inviolable right to life proper to every individual; they thus deny the equality of everyone before the law" (*Evangelium Vitae*, no. 72). What is at stake here is nothing less than the indivisible truth about the human person on which the founding fathers staked your nation's claim to independence. The life of a country is much more than its material development and its power in the world. A nation needs a "soul." It needs the wisdom and courage to overcome the moral ills and spiritual temptations inherent in its march through history. In union with all those who favor a "culture of life" over a "culture of death," Catholics, and especially Catholic legislators, must continue to make their voices heard in the formulation of cultural, economic, political, and legislative projects which, "with respect for all and in keeping with democratic principles, will contribute to the building of a society in which the dignity of each person is recognized and the lives of all are defended and enhanced" (*Evangelium Vitae*, no. 90). Democracy stands or falls with the values which it embodies and promotes (cf. *Evangelium Vitae*, no. 70). In defending life you are defending an original and vital part of the vision on which your country was built. America must become, again, a hospitable society, in which every unborn child and every handicapped or terminally ill person is cherished and enjoys the protection of the law.

7. Dear brother bishops, Catholic moral teaching is an essential part of our heritage of faith; we must see to it that it is faithfully transmitted\ and take appropriate measures to guard the faithful from the deceit of opinions which dissent from it (cf. *Veritatis Splendor*, nos. 26 and 113). Although the Church often appears as a sign of contradiction, in defending the whole moral law firmly and humbly she is upholding truths which are indispensable for the good of humanity and for the safeguarding of civilization itself. Our teaching must be clear; it must recognize the drama of the human condition, in which we all struggle with sin and in which we must all strive, with the help of grace, to embrace

the good (cf. *Gaudium et Spes*, no. 13). Our task as teachers is to "show the inviting splendor of that truth which is Jesus Christ himself" (*Veritatis Splendor*, no. 83). Living the moral life involves holding fast to the very person of Jesus, partaking of his life and destiny, sharing in his free and loving obedience to the will of the Father.

May your fidelity to the Lord and the responsibility for his Church which he has given you make you personally vigilant to ensure that only sound doctrine of faith and morals is presented as Catholic teaching. Invoking the intercession of Our Lady upon your ministry, I cordially impart my apostolic blessing to you and to the priests, religious, and lay faithful of your dioceses.

FROM THE VATICAN, OCTOBER 2, 1998

Joannes Paulus PP. II

GREETING
OF THE BISHOPS
Region XII

Your Holiness:

On behalf of the bishops of Region XII and two from Region XIII of the National Conference of Catholic Bishops, I greet you in the name of the Lord.

On your historic first trip to Alaska in 1981, I welcomed you literally to the end of the earth, noting, "No future pope will travel further from the Eternal City of Rome, unless he chooses a spaceship to the moon." The astronauts did not remain on the moon long enough to extend you that invitation, an invitation which many feel would be very tempting to Your Holiness.

In your twenty-year pontificate, however, you have traveled almost three times the distance to the moon, fulfilling the words in St. Luke's Gospel: "I have made you a light to the nations, so that my salvation shall reach the end of the world."

As you have circled the world, you described yourself as a pilgrim of faith responding to the charge that Jesus gave to Peter: "Strengthen your brothers." By your word, Your Holiness, you have strengthened us. By your trips to the United States, in which you insisted on greeting us individually, you have strengthened us. On our *Ad Limina* visits you have welcomed us literally into your home. Humanly and spiritually you are a brother to us.

We thank you, Holy Father, and express our love for you in return.

In the northwestern part of the United States, which includes Alaska, Idaho, Montana, Oregon, and Washington, the general population is described as "unchurched." This is accurate but there are signs of change as new immigrants bring with them their practice of the faith, specifically Filipino, Hispanic, Vietnamese, Korean, and others. How multicultural we have become is exemplified by the native village of Barrow, Alaska, the northernmost town of the United States. It has a Mexican restaurant and three hundred Filipino residents.

We are still young churches in a culture that is dominantly secular. Fostering vocations to the priesthood and religious life is difficult. You assist us mightily by your repeated calls to the youth of the world and by your embracing of them in the World Youth Days.

The number of priests and religious has always been small. We cover vast territories where travel is difficult and time-consuming. Throughout the early years, laity were integral to the building up of the local church and to making the Church a vital presence in the general community. It was not surprising to us, therefore, that the impetus given by the Holy Spirit through the Second Vatican Council for increased involvement of the laity in the apostolate of the Church has found a generous, and even excited, response among our lay people, men, women, and youth.

There are tensions arising within the Church as a result of the rapid expansion of lay participation, but the vast majority of laity understand the ministries and roles to which the Church calls them, as well as the indispensable role of the ordained priest. Where there is an interplay of training and prayerful reflection, the tensions are not an obstacle to growth. When tensions seem difficult, we heed the words of the patroness of the mission, St. Therese of Lisieux, whose feast we just celebrated: "For those who trust in God, all is well."

Perhaps it is because of our not being intimidated by territorial distances and shortages of personnel that the dioceses of the Northwest have reached out to the Russian Far East, each in its own way. In this we strive to be supportive of your own overtures to the Orthodox world.

In our "unchurched" area we have found a disposition among differing churches to ecumenical and interreligious relationships. These relationships have been strengthened by your call for reconciliation in preparation for the year 2000. In this world of instant and graphic stories of international and domestic violence we all sense how urgent it is that we seek reconciliation together.

Intertwined with reconciliation is your vision of a New Jerusalem. You have called us to remember the Holocaust. You voice your burning desire to visit the Holy Land. You reflect the vision of St. John in the Book of Revelation in your desire to show the world a New Jerusalem: "Jerusalem, the Holy City coming down from God . . . with the 12 gates . . . and over the gates the names of the 12 tribes of Israel. . . . The city stood on the 12 foundation stones . . . each one bearing the name of one of the 12 apostles of the Lamb." Twelve tribes and twelve apostles. We pray with you that they may be one.

A trip to the moon, Your Holiness, would be for the world only a symbolic journey in time. A trip to the Holy Land will be truly reconciliation for eternity. We pray that you will be able to make that trip. We congratulate you on your twentieth anniversary as our Holy Father. We ask the Holy Spirit to enlighten and strengthen you. We ask your blessing on us and on our people.

MOST REV. FRANCIS T. HURLEY
ARCHBISHOP OF ANCHORAGE

ADDRESS OF
POPE JOHN PAUL II
Region XII

Dear Brother Bishops:

1. With fraternal love in the Lord I welcome you, the pastors of the Church in the northwestern United States, on the occasion of your *Ad Limina* visit. This series of visits by the bishops of your country to the tombs of the apostles Peter and Paul, and to the Successor of Peter and his collaborators in the service of the universal Church, is taking place while the whole people of God is preparing to celebrate the Great Jubilee of the Year 2000 and enter a new Christian millennium. The two thousandth anniversary of the birth of the Savior is a call to all Christ's followers to seek a genuine conversion to God and a great advance in holiness. Since the liturgy is such a central part of the Christian life, I wish today to consider some aspects of the liturgical renewal so vigorously promoted by the Second Vatican Council as the prime agent of the wider renewal of Catholic life.

To look back over what has been done in the field of liturgical renewal in the years since the council is, first, to see many reasons for giving heartfelt thanks and praise to the Most Holy Trinity for the marvelous awareness which has developed among the faithful of their role and responsibility in this priestly work of Christ and his Church. It is also to realize that not all changes have always and everywhere been accompanied by the necessary explanation and catechesis; as a result, in some cases there has been a misunderstanding of the very nature of the liturgy, leading to abuses, polarization, and sometimes even grave scandal. After the experience of more than thirty years of liturgical renewal, we are well placed to assess both the strengths and weaknesses of what has been done, in order more confidently to plot our course into the future which God has in mind for his cherished people.

2. The challenge now is to move beyond whatever misunderstandings there have been and to reach the proper point of balance, especially by entering more deeply into the contemplative dimension of worship, which includes the sense of awe, reverence, and adoration which are fundamental attitudes in our relationship with God. This will happen only if we recognize that the liturgy has dimensions both local and universal, time-bound and eternal, horizontal and vertical, subjective and objective. It is precisely these tensions which give to Catholic worship its distinctive character.

The universal Church is united in the one great act of praise; but it is always the worship of a particular community in a particular culture. It is the eternal worship of heaven, but it is also steeped in time. It gathers and builds a human community, but it is also "the worship of the divine majesty" (*Sacrosanctum Concilium*, no. 33). It is subjective in that it depends radically upon what the worshipers bring to it; but it is objective in that it transcends them as the priestly act of Christ himself, to which he associates us but which ultimately does not depend upon us (ibid., no. 7). This is why it is so important that liturgical law be respected. The priest, who is the servant of the liturgy, not its inventor or producer, has a particular responsibility in this regard, lest he empty liturgy of its true meaning or obscure its sacred character.

The core of the mystery of Christian worship is the sacrifice of Christ offered to the Father and the work of the risen Christ who sanctifies his people through the liturgical signs. It is therefore essential that in seeking to enter more deeply into the contemplative depths of worship the inexhaustible mystery of the priesthood of Jesus Christ be fully acknowledged and respected.

While all the baptized share in that one priesthood of Christ, not all share in it in the same manner. The ministerial priesthood, rooted in apostolic succession, confers on the ordained priest faculties and responsibilities which are different from those of the laity but which are at the service of the common priesthood and are directed at the unfolding of the baptismal grace of all Christians (cf. *Catechism of the Catholic Church*, no. 1547). The priest therefore is not just one who presides, but one who acts in the person of Christ.

3. Only by being radically faithful to this doctrinal foundation can we avoid one-dimensional and unilateral interpretations of the council's teaching. The sharing of all the baptized in the one priesthood of Jesus Christ is the key to understanding the council's call for "full, conscious and active participation" in the liturgy (*Sacrosanctum Concilium*, no. 14). Full participation certainly means that every member of the community has a part to play in the liturgy; and in this respect a great deal has been achieved in parishes and communities across your land. But full participation does not mean that everyone does everything, since this would lead to a clericalizing of the laity and a laicizing of the priesthood, and this was not what the council had in mind. The liturgy, like the Church, is intended to be hierarchical and polyphonic, respecting the different roles assigned by Christ and allowing all the different voices to blend in one great hymn of praise.

Active participation certainly means that, in gesture, word, song, and service, all the members of the community take part in an act of worship, which is anything but inert or passive. Yet active participation does not preclude the active passivity of silence, stillness, and listening: indeed, it demands it. Worshipers are not passive, for instance, when listening to the readings or the homily, or following the prayers of the celebrant and the chants and music of the liturgy. These are experiences of silence and stillness, but they are in their own way profoundly active. In a culture which neither favors nor fosters meditative quiet, the art of interior listening is learned only with difficulty. Here we see how the liturgy, though it must always be properly inculturated, must also be countercultural.

Conscious participation calls for the entire community to be properly instructed in the mysteries of the liturgy, lest the experience of worship degenerate into a form of ritualism. But it does not mean a constant attempt within the liturgy itself to make the implicit explicit, since this often leads to a verbosity and informality which are alien to the Roman rite and end by trivializing the act of worship.

Nor does it mean the suppression of all subconscious experience, which is vital in a liturgy which thrives on symbols that speak to the subconscious just as they speak to the conscious. The use of the vernacular has certainly opened up the treasures of the liturgy to all who take part, but this does not mean that the Latin language, and especially the chants which are so superbly adapted to the genius of the Roman rite, should be wholly abandoned. If subconscious experience is ignored in worship, an affective and devotional vacuum is created and the liturgy can become not only too verbal but also too cerebral. Yet the Roman rite is again distinctive in the balance it strikes between a spareness and a richness of emotion: it feeds the heart and the mind, the body and the soul.

It has been written with good reason that in the history of the Church all true renewal has been linked to a rereading of the church fathers. And what is true in general is true of the liturgy in particular. The fathers were pastors with a burning zeal for the task of spreading the Gospel; and therefore they were profoundly interested in all the dimensions of worship, leaving us some of the most significant and enduring texts of the Christian tradition, which are anything but the result of a barren aestheticism.

The fathers were ardent preachers, and it is hard to imagine that there can be an effective renewal of Catholic preaching, as the council wished, without sufficient familiarity with the patristic tradition. The council promoted a move to a homiletic mode of preaching which would, like the fathers, expound the biblical text in a way which opens its inexhaustible riches to the faithful.

The importance that preaching has assumed in Catholic worship since the council means that priests and deacons should be trained to make good use of the Bible. But this also involves familiarity with the whole patristic, theological, and moral tradition, as well as a penetrating knowledge of their communities and of society in general. Otherwise, the impression is given of a teaching without roots and without the universal application inherent in the gospel message. The excellent synthesis of the Church's doctrinal wealth contained in the *Catechism of the Catholic Church* has yet to be more widely felt as an influence on Catholic preaching.

4. It is essential to keep clearly in mind that the liturgy is intimately linked to the Church's mission to evangelize. If the two do not go hand in hand, both will falter. Insofar as developments in liturgical renewal are superficial or unbalanced, our energies for a new evangelization will be compromised; and insofar as our vision falls short of the new evangelization, our liturgical renewal will be reduced to external and possibly unsound adaptation. The Roman rite has always been a form of worship that looks to mission. This is why it is comparatively brief: there was much to be done outside the Church; and this is why we have the dismissal "Ite, missa est," which gives us the term "Mass": the community is sent forth to evangelize the world in obedience to Christ's command (cf. Mt 28:19-20).

As pastors, you are fully aware of the great thirst for God and the desire for prayer which people feel today. The World Youth Day in Denver stands out as evidence that the younger generation of Americans too yearns for a deep and demanding faith in Jesus Christ. They want to have an active role in the Church and to be sent out in the name of Christ to evangelize and transform the world around them.

Young people are ready to commit themselves to the gospel message if it is presented in all its nobility and liberating force.

They will continue to take an active part in the liturgy if they experience it as capable of leading them to a deep personal relationship with God; and it is from this experience that there will come priestly and religious vocations marked by true evangelical and missionary energy. In this sense, the young are summoning the whole Church to take the next step in implementing the vision of worship which the council has bequeathed to us. Unburdened by the ideological agenda of an earlier time, they are able to speak simply and directly of their desire to experience God, especially in prayer both public and private. In listening to them, dear brothers, we may well hear "what the Spirit is saying to the churches" (Rv 2:11 [NRSV]).

5. In our preparation for the Great Jubilee of the Year 2000, the year 1999 will be devoted to the person of the Father and to the celebration of his merciful love. Initiatives for next year should draw particular attention to the nature of the Christian life as "a great pilgrimage to the house of the Father, whose unconditional love for every human creature, and in particular for the 'prodigal son,' we discover anew each day" (*Tertio Millennio Adveniente*, no. 49). At the core of this experience of pilgrimage is our journey as sinners into the unfathomable depths of the Church's liturgy, the liturgy of creation, the liturgy of heaven—all of which are in the end the worship of Jesus Christ, the Eternal Priest, in whom the Church and all creation are drawn into the life of the Most Holy Trinity, our true home. That is the purpose of all our worship and all our evangelizing.

At the very heart of the worshiping community, we find the Mother of Christ and Mother of the Church, who, from the depths of her contemplative faith, brings forth the good news, which is Jesus Christ himself. Together with you I pray that American Catholics when they celebrate the liturgy will have in their hearts the same song that she sang: "My being proclaims the greatness of the Lord, my spirit finds joy in God my Saviour. . . . God who is mighty has done great things for me, holy is his name" (Lk 1:46-50 [NAB 1970]). In entrusting the priests, religious, and lay faithful of your dioceses to the Blessed Mother's loving protection, I cordially impart my apostolic blessing.

FROM THE VATICAN, OCTOBER 9, 1998

Joannes Paulus II

GREETING
OF THE BISHOPS
Region XIII

Your Holiness, John Paul II:

It is with joy that we, the archbishops and bishops of the two provinces of Santa Fe and Denver and the bishops of Salt Lake City and El Paso in the southwest and Rocky Mountain states of the United States of America, gather with you in this city made holy by the ministry and martyrdom of the glorious apostles Peter and Paul.

Our *Ad Limina* visit this year holds special significance for us Catholics of the Southwest: It was exactly four hundred years ago that the Catholic faith, built upon the apostles, was established in Santa Fe, N.M. In time, the Church spread to the areas which we now serve as bishops. While this is but a short time when compared to the two thousand-year history of the Church, for us in the United States, it marks the oldest permanent establishment of the Catholic faith in our country.

This planting of the faith began with the seeds of struggle: the struggle of the Spanish colonists and Franciscan missionaries to maintain their Catholic faith in an isolated and harsh environment and the struggle to preach the Gospel to the Native Americans of the region. In this struggle there were often mistakes and disappointments. Yet by the grace of God, the Catholic faith has endured and flourished in our land, bearing a rich harvest of faith in the archdioceses and dioceses we serve.

These struggles have not all been in ancient times. Some have been in our own day. I know, Holy Father, that you are aware of the painful difficulties that some of us faced but a few years ago. They were challenging times. However, we had trust in the Lord who is ever able to bring good out of evil. These difficulties became an occasion for us to examine our consciences, to humbly admit our own sins and failings, and to recommit ourselves to Jesus our Savior and the spread of his kingdom.

Thus, despite the trials that we endure in our episcopal ministry, I am pleased to tell you that the faithful fill our churches in ever greater numbers, that works of mercy and evangelization are flourishing, and, a most special joy to me, we have seen a dramatic increase in vocations in several of our dioceses. In all this we thank God, who rescues and sustains his people. God continues to grant a rich harvest of faith for the Catholic Church in our dioceses.

We wish to thank you for your tireless efforts in guiding the Church and in giving us encouragement in the exercise of the office of bishop. In particular do we express gratitude for your pastorally sensitive apostolic letter, *Dies Domini*, on the observance of Sunday eucharist. This document on the proper observance and celebration of the day of the Lord is very well received and is bearing much fruit in the spiritual lives of our people.

Despite the blessings, we also experience serious difficulties in the materialism and secularism which abound in our country. We are facing a severe problem in the shortage of priests in our churches just as the rest of our country does. A growing number of parishes are without a resident priest in many parts of Region XIII. Nevertheless, we continue to promote vocations to priesthood and religious life, trusting that the Lord will not forget our urgent need for priests.

We recall with wonderful memories your fruitful visit to Denver for World Youth Day in 1993. Our Lord truly used you as his instrument in a powerful way as you encouraged large numbers of young people in the practice of the Catholic faith. Our youth love you and are grateful for your prayers and support.

On the occasion of the cuarto centennial of the Catholic faith in the Southwest, we together with all the clergy, religious, and faithful under our care, wish to reaffirm our love and loyalty to you, the chief shepherd of the Church, and to the apostolic Catholic faith which you embody in the office of Peter. As we ask your blessings upon the churches which we serve, we assure you of our constant prayers for your health and well-being and ask that God will continue to grant you wisdom, strength, and peace as you nobly shepherd the universal Church.

MOST REV. MICHAEL J. SHEEHAN
ARCHBISHOP OF SANTA FE

ADDRESS OF
POPE JOHN PAUL II
Region XIII

Dear Brother Bishops:

1. With great joy I greet you, the pastors of the church in the states of Colorado, Wyoming, Utah, Arizona, and New Mexico. Your *Ad Limina* visit, by bringing you to "see Peter" (cf. Gal 1:18), is meant to be, in the life of the particular churches over which you preside, an opportunity "to strengthen unity in the same faith, hope and charity, and more and more recognize and treasure that immense heritage of spiritual and moral wealth that the whole church, joined with the bishop of Rome by the bond of communion, has spread throughout the world" (*Pastor Bonus*, Appendix I, no. 3).

In this series of meetings with the bishops of the United States, I have emphasized that the faithful and committed implementation of the teachings of the Second Vatican Council is the path indicated by the Holy Spirit for the whole Church to prepare for the Great Jubilee of the Year 2000 and the beginning of the new millennium. The renewal of Christian life which was at the forefront of the council's work is the same goal which guided Pope John XXIII to advocate a revision of the *Code of Canon Law* (cf. Address to Roman Cardinals, January 25, 1959), a desire reaffirmed by the council fathers (cf. *Christus Dominus*, no. 44). After much labor this revision bore fruit in the new *Code of Canon Law* promulgated in 1983 and the *Code of Canons of the Eastern Churches* promulgated in 1990. Today I wish to reflect on some aspects of your ministry in relation to the place of law in the Church.

2. The immediate purpose of the revision of the code was to ensure that it embodied the ecclesiology of the Second Vatican Council. And, given that the council's teaching aimed at stirring new energies for a new evangelization, it is clear that the revision of the code belongs to that series of graces and gifts which the Holy Spirit has poured out so abundantly on the ecclesial community so that, in fidelity to Christ, it will enter the next millennium seeking to give witness to the truth, to rescue and not to sit in judgment, to serve and not to be served (cf. *Tertio Millennio Adveniente*, no. 56).

To understand more of the link between law and evangelization we need to consider the biblical roots of law in the Church. The Old Testament insists that the Torah is the greatest of God's gifts to Israel, and each year the Jewish people still celebrate the feast called the Rejoicing of the Torah. The Torah is a great gift because it opens to people in every time and place the path of an ever new exodus. For us, just as for Israel, the question is this: Long ago our ancestors came forth from the slavery of Egypt, but how are we now to come forth from the slavery which afflicts us, from the Egypt of our own time and place? The biblical answer is: You will find freedom if you obey this divine law. At the heart of biblical revelation, therefore, there lies the mystery of a liberating obedience, which reaches its supreme expression in the crucified Christ who was "obedient unto death" (Phil 2:8 [RSV]). Ultimate obedience made possible the definitive liberation of Easter.

In the Church, then, the purpose of law is the defense and promotion of the "glorious liberty of the children of God" (Rom 8:21 [RSV]); this is the good news which Christ sends us to bring to the world. To see the law as spiritually liberating runs against the grain of a certain understanding of law in western culture, which tends to view law as a necessary evil, a kind of control required to guard fragile human rights and restrain wayward human passions, but which would disappear in the best of all possible worlds. This is not the biblical view; nor can it be the Church's view.

Authority in the Church, being a sacred ministry at the service of the proclamation of God's word and the sanctification of the faithful, can only be understood as a means for the development of the Christian life in accordance with the radical demands of the Gospel. Ecclesiastical law gives form to the community or social body of the Church, always with a view to that supreme objective which is the salvation of souls (cf. canons 747, 978, 1752). Since this ultimate end is attained above all through the newness of life in the Spirit, the provisions of the law aim at safeguarding and fostering Christian life by regulating the exercise of faith, the sacraments, charity, and ecclesiastical government.

3. The common good which the law protects and promotes is not a mere external order, but the sum of those conditions which make possible the spiritual and internal reality of communion with God and communion between the members of the Church. Consequently, as a basic rule, ecclesiastical laws bind in conscience. In other words, obedience to the law is not a mere external submission to authority but a means of growing in faith, charity, and holiness, under the guidance and by the grace of the Holy Spirit. In this sense canon law has particular features which distinguish it from civil law and which preclude the application of the legal structures of civil society to the Church without the necessary modifications. Appreciation of these particularities is necessary in order to overcome some of the difficulties which have arisen in recent times regarding the understanding, interpretation, and application of canon law.

Among these particularities is the pastoral character of law and of the exercise of justice in the Church. In fact, the pastoral character of canon law is the key to the correct understanding of canonical equity, that attitude of mind and spirit which tempers the rigor of the law in order to foster a higher good. In the Church, equity is an expression of charity in the truth, aiming at a higher justice which coincides with the supernatural good of the individual and of the community. Equity, then, should characterize the work of the pastor and the judge, who must continually model themselves on the Good Shepherd, "consoling those who have been struck down, guiding those who have erred, recognizing the rights of those who have been injured, calumniated or unjustly humiliated" (Paul VI, Address to the Roman Rota, February 8, 1973).

Elements such as dispensation, tolerance, exempting or excusing causes, and *epikeia* are to be understood not as diminishing the force of law but as complementing it, since they actually guarantee that the law's fundamental purpose is secured. Likewise, ecclesiastical censures are not vindictive but medicinal, inasmuch as they aim at bringing about the conversion of the sinner. All law in the Church has truth and charity as its constitutive elements and its primary motivating principles.

4. The code specifies the duties of bishops regarding the setting up of tribunals and their activity. It is not enough to ensure that diocesan tribunals have the personnel and means to function properly. Your responsibility as bishops—about which I encourage you to be especially vigilant—is to ensure that diocesan tribunals exercise faithfully the ministry of truth and justice.

In my own ministry I have always felt the weight of this particular responsibility. As the successor of Peter I have reason to be deeply grateful to my collaborators in the various tribunals of the Apostolic See: especially the Apostolic Penitentiary, the Supreme Tribunal of the Apostolic Signatura, and the Tribunal of the Roman Rota, which help me in that part of my ministry which deals with the proper administration of justice.

Canon law touches on every aspect of the Church's life and therefore imposes upon bishops a wide range of responsibilities, but it is undoubtedly in the area of marriage that these responsibilities are felt most acutely and are most complex. The indissolubility of marriage is a teaching that comes from Christ himself, and the first duty of pastors and pastoral workers is therefore to help couples overcome whatever difficulties arise.

The referral of matrimonial cases to the tribunal should be a last resort. Great care must be taken when explaining to the faithful what a declaration of nullity is, in order to avoid the danger of its being conceived as divorce under a different name. The tribunal exercises a ministry of truth: its purpose is "to ascertain whether or not the facts exist that by natural, divine or ecclesiastical law invalidate the marriage, in order to be able to issue a true and just sentence concerning the alleged nonexistence of the marriage bond" (Address to the Roman Rota, February 4, 1980, no. 2).

The process leading to a judicial decision about the alleged nullity of marriage should demonstrate two aspects of the Church's pastoral mission. First, it should manifest clearly the desire to be faithful to the Lord's teaching concerning the permanent nature of sacramental marriage. Secondly, it should be inspired by genuine pastoral concern for those who seek the ministry of the tribunal in order to clarify their status in the Church.

5. Justice demands that the work of tribunals be carried out conscientiously and in strict observance of canonical directions and procedures. As moderators of your diocesan tribunals, you have the duty to ensure that the officials of the tribunal are suitably qualified (cf. canons 1420, 4; 1421, 3; 1428, 2; 1435), possessing a doctorate or at least a licentiate in canon law. Where this is not the case, they need to be properly dispensed by the Apostolic Signatura after receiving specialized training for their position.

In regard to the officials of the tribunal, I urge you in particular to see that the defender of the bond is diligent in presenting and expounding all that can reasonably be argued against the nullity of the marriage (cf. canon 1432). Bishops whose tribunals handle cases in second instance should ensure that their tribunals treat their competence seriously, not acting merely as an almost automatic confirmation of the judgment of the tribunal of first instance.

Both parties in a marriage case have rights which must be scrupulously respected. These include the right to be heard for the formulation of the doubt, the right to know on what grounds the case will be tried, the right to name witnesses, the right to inspect the acts, the right to know and rebut the arguments of the other party and of the defender of the bond, and to receive a copy of the final sentence. The parties are to be informed of the ways in which they may challenge the definitive sentence, including the right to appeal to the Tribunal of the Roman Rota in second instance.

In regard to cases tried on the basis of psychic incapacity, that is, on the basis of some serious psychic anomaly which renders a person incapable of contracting a valid marriage (cf. canon 1095), the tribunal is to make use of the services of an expert in psychology or psychiatry who shares a Christian anthropology in accordance with the Church's understanding of the human person (cf. Address to the Roman Rota, February 5, 1987).

A canonical process must never be seen as a mere formality to be observed or a set of rules to be manipulated. The judge may not pass sentence in favor of the nullity of a marriage if he has not first acquired the moral certainty of the existence of this nullity; probability alone is not sufficient to decide a case (cf. ibid., no. 6; canon 1608).

Moral certainty—which is not just probability or subjective conviction—"is characterized on the positive side by the exclusion of well-founded or reasonable doubt. On the negative side, it does admit the absolute possibility of the contrary and in this it differs from absolute certainty" (Pius XII, Address to the Roman Rota, October 1, 1942, no. 1). Moral certainty proceeds from a multitude of indications and demonstrations which, taken separately, may not be decisive, but which taken together can exclude any reasonable doubt. If the judge cannot reach moral certainty in the canonical trial, he must find in favor of the validity of the matrimonial bond (cf. canon 1608, 3 and 4): marriage enjoys the favor of the law.

6. Dear brother bishops, the purpose of these brief considerations is to encourage you in overseeing the faithful application of canonical legislation: This is essential if the Church is to show herself ever more equal to the task of carrying out her salvific mission (cf. apostolic constitution *Sacrae Disciplinae Leges*).

A deeper appreciation of the importance of canon law in the life of the Church and the implementation of measures to guarantee a more effective and conscientious administration of justice must be a central concern of your episcopal ministry. Fidelity to ecclesiastical law should be a vital part of the renewal of your particular churches. It is a condition for unleashing new energies for evangelization as we approach the third Christian millennium.

I entrust your pastoral efforts in this regard to the maternal intercession of Mary, Mirror of Justice, and to you and the priests, religious, and lay faithful of your dioceses, I gladly impart my apostolic blessing.

FROM THE VATICAN, OCTOBER 17, 1998

Joannes Paulus II

GREETING
OF THE BISHOPS
Region I

Most Holy Father,

In the name of Archbishop Daniel A. Cronin, archbishop of Hartford; Bishop Basil Losten, bishop of the Ukrainian Catholic Church of Stamford; Bishop John Elya, eparch of the Melchite Eparchy of Newton; and the other bishops of Region I of the United States, I express our profound gratitude for the audiences which you have granted us, for the gracious hospitality of your table, and particularly for the opportunity to join with you in the celebration of the eucharistic sacrifice.

What a fitting way to end this *Ad Limina* visit through the celebration of the eucharist: the source and summit of our *communio*.

The territory of the eleven Latin dioceses of Region I comprised but one diocese in 1808 when the Diocese of Boston was established. Three other dioceses were established in that same year: New York, Philadelphia, and Bardstown, Ky. In 1808, there were only several thousand Catholics and a handful of priests in all of New England. Today we are here as bishops of eleven vibrant dioceses as well as two jurisdictions of Eastern churches numbering more than three million Catholics.

Thank you, Holy Father, for confirming your brothers in the faith. We note with gratitude your three most recent encyclicals: *Veritatis Splendor*, *Evangelium Vitae*, and *Fides et Ratio*. We are delighted to have been in Rome for the twentieth anniversary of your election to the chair of Peter. The faithful whom we serve join us in pledging you our prayers, love, and fidelity.

CARDINAL BERNARD F. LAW
ARCHBISHOP OF BOSTON

ADDRESS OF
POPE JOHN PAUL II
Region I

Dear Cardinal Law,
Dear Brother Bishops:

1. I warmly greet you, the bishops of New England, comprising the ecclesiastical provinces of Boston and Hartford. During this year, I have had the spiritual joy of meeting practically all the pastors of the Church in the United States of America, representing more than two hundred jurisdictions, including those of the Eastern-rite Catholic churches. As we come to the end of this series of *Ad Limina* visits, I "give thanks to God always for you because of the grace which has been given you in Christ Jesus, that in every way you have been enriched in him" (cf. 1 Cor 1:4-5). We have prayed together and listened to one another, seeking to take stock of all the good which the Holy Spirit inspires among the people of God in your country. Apart from strengthening the bonds of communion between us, these visits have enabled us to reflect, in an atmosphere of pilgrimage and prayerful calm, on the opportunities for evangelization and apostolate which lie before the Church in the United States in the light of the teaching of the Second Vatican Council and the approaching Great Jubilee of the Year 2000.

2. Occasions such as the great jubilee remind us of all that God has done in history, and they prompt us to look to the future, confident in the Lord's promise that he will be with us always, "to the close of the age" (Mt 28:20 [RSV]). Christians know that time is neither a mere suc-

cession of days, months, and years, nor a cosmic cycle of eternal return. Time is a great drama with a beginning and an end, authored and directed by God's providential care: "Within the dimension of time the world was created; within it the history of salvation unfolds, finding its culmination in the 'fullness of time' of the Incarnation, and its goal in the glorious return of the Son of God at the end of time" (*Tertio Millennio Adveniente*, no. 10). The Easter vigil reminds us that the resurrection is "the true fulcrum of history, to which the mystery of the world's origin and its final destiny leads" (*Dies Domini*, no. 2). Only in the light of the Risen Christ do we come to understand the true meaning of our personal pilgrimage through time to our eternal destiny. This is the message which the Church must proclaim today and always.

She does so above all in the liturgy, which celebrates the history of salvation and is the privileged place for our encounter with the Father and the one whom he has sent, Jesus Christ. She does so in her kerygma and catechesis, which make known the saving teaching of the Gospel in dialogue with the human heart's profound aspiration for something divine and eternal, something supremely good that will not slip away. And she does so in her works of charity, which seek to heal the brokenness of human lives by the healing touch of Christian love.

3. In my talks to the bishops—addressed not only to the bishops present on each occasion but to your entire conference—I have tried to reflect on aspects of your episcopal ministry which can open the door to the great springtime of Christianity which God is preparing as we enter the third Christian millennium, and of which we can already see the first signs (cf. *Redemptoris Missio*, no. 86). Together we have conversed about many features of the life of the Catholic community in the United States, blessed by the genuine holiness of so many of its members, marked by a deep thirst for justice, steadfast and active in all the various forms of Christian service.

As bishops you are well aware of the strengths of your people. Like the wise man of the Gospel, you must calculate how with the energies and means available you can face the urgent needs of the present time (cf. Lk 14:31). Today I believe the Lord is saying to us all: do not hesitate, do not be afraid to engage the good fight of the faith (cf. 1 Tm 6:12). When we preach the liberating message of Jesus Christ, we are offering the words of life to the world (cf. Jn 6:68). Our prophetic witness is an urgent and essential service not just to the Catholic community but to the whole human family. For in the Gospel the true story of the world is told, its history and its future, which is life within the communion of the Holy Trinity.

At the end of the second millennium humanity stands at a kind of crossroads. As pastors responsible for the life of the Church, we need to meditate deeply on the signs of a new spiritual crisis, whose dangers are apparent not only at the personal level but regarding civilization itself (cf. *Evangelium Vitae*, no. 68). If this crisis deepens, utilitarianism will increasingly reduce human beings to objects for manipulation. If the moral truth revealed in the dignity of the human person does not discipline and direct the explosive energies of technology, a new era of barbarism, rather than a springtime of hope, may well follow this century of tears (cf. Speech to the United Nations, October 5, 1995, no. 18).

In addressing the United Nations General Assembly in 1995, I proposed that in order to recover our hope and our trust on the threshold of a new century "we must regain sight of that transcendent horizon of possibility to which the soul of man aspires" (ibid., no. 16). Because the spiritual crisis of our times is in fact a flight from the transcendent mystery of God, it is at the same time a flight from the truth about the human person, God's noblest creation on earth.

The culture of our day seeks to build without reference to the architect, ignoring the biblical warning: "Unless the LORD builds the house, those who build it labor in vain" (Ps 127:1 [NRSV]). In doing so, a certain part of contemporary culture misses the depth and richness of the human mystery, and life itself is thereby impoverished, being divested of meaning and joy. No demand on our ministry is more urgent than the "new evangelization" needed to satisfy the spiritual hunger of our times. We must not hesitate before the challenge of communicating the joy of being Christian, of being "in Christ," in the state of grace with God, and of being united with the Church. This is what can truly satisfy the human heart and its aspiration to freedom.

4. Nowhere is the contrast between the gospel vision and contemporary culture more obvious than in the dramatic conflict between the culture of life and the culture of death. I do not wish to end this series of meetings without once more thanking the bishops for their leadership and advocacy in support of human life, particularly the lives of the most vulnerable.

The Church in your country reaches out in the defense and promotion of human life and human dignity in numerous ways. Through countless organizations and agencies she is an immensely generous provider of social services to the poor; active in support of laws more favorable to the immigrant; present in the public debate on capital punishment, aware that in the modern state the cases in which the execution of an offender is an absolute necessity are very rare, if not practically nonexistent (cf. *Evangelium Vitae*, no. 56; *Catechism of the Catholic Church*, no. 2267).

At the same time, you rightly underscore the priority that must be given to the fundamental right to life of the unborn and to opposition to euthanasia and physician-assisted suicide. The witness of so many United States Catholics—including countless young people—in the service of "the Gospel of life" is a sure sign of hope for the future and a reason for us to be thankful to the Holy Spirit who inspires so much good among the faithful.

5. In response to the spiritual crisis of our times, I am convinced that there is a radical need for a healing of the mind as well as of the heart. The violent history of this century is due in no small part to the closure of reason to the existence of ultimate and objective truth. The result has been a pervasive skepticism and relativism, which have not led to a more "mature" humanity but to much despair and irrationality.

In the encyclical letter *Fides et Ratio*, published only last week, I wished to defend the capacity of human reason to know the truth. This confidence in reason is an integral part of the Catholic intellectual tradition, but it needs reaffirming today in the face of a widespread and doctrinaire doubt about our ability to answer the fundamental questions: Who am I? Where have I come from and where am I going to? Why is there evil? What is there after this life? (cf. *Fides et Ratio*, nos. 3 and 5).

Many people have been led to believe that the only truths are those which can be demonstrated by experience or scientific experimentation. The result is a tendency to reduce the domain of rational inquiry to technological, instrumental, utilitarian, functional, and sociological dimensions of things. A relativistic and pragmatic vision of truth has emerged. An undifferentiated plurality, based on the assumption that all positions are equally valid, replaces a legitimate pluralism of positions in dialogue (cf. ibid., no. 5).

One of the most striking indications of the contemporary lack of confidence in truth is the tendency found among some to rest content with partial and provisional truths, "no longer seeking to ask . . . the meaning and ultimate foundation of human, personal and social existence" (ibid.). By being satisfied with experimental and incomplete knowledge, reason fails to do justice to the mystery of the human person, made for the truth and deeply desirous of knowing the truth.

The consequences for the faith of this widespread attitude are serious. If reason cannot attain ultimate truths, faith loses its reasonable and intelligible character and is reduced to the realm of the non-definable, the sentimental, and the irrational. The outcome is fideism. Detached from its relationship to human reason, faith loses its public and universal validity and is limited to the subjective and private sphere. In the end, theological faith is destroyed.

On the basis of these concerns, I considered it important to write the encyclical letter *Fides et Ratio*, addressed to you, the bishops of the Church, the principal witnesses to divine and Catholic truth (cf. *Lumen Gentium*, no. 25). My wish is to encourage you, as bishops, always to keep open the horizon of your ministry, beyond the immediate tasks of your daily pastoral toil, to that deep and universal thirst for the truth which is found in every human heart.

6. The dialogue of the Church with contemporary culture is part of your *"diakonia of the truth"* (*Fides et Ratio*, no. 2). You must do all you can to raise the level of philosophical and theological reflection, not only in seminaries and Catholic institutions (cf. ibid., no. 62), but also among Catholic intellectuals and all those who seek a deeper understanding of reality.

As we approach the new millennium, the Church's defense of the human person requires a firm and open defense of the capacity of human reason to reach definitive truths concerning God, concerning man himself, concerning freedom, and concerning ethical behavior. Only through reasoned reflection, open to the fundamental questions of existence and free from reductive presuppositions, can society discover sure points of reference on which to build a secure foundation for the lives of individuals and communities.

Faith and reason in cooperation manifest the grandeur of the human being, "who can find fulfilment only in choosing to enter the truth, to make a home under the shade of Wisdom and dwell there" (ibid., no. 107). The Church's long intellectual tradition is born of her confidence in the goodness of creation and the ability of reason to grasp metaphysical and moral truths. Collaboration between faith and reason, and the continued involvement of Christian thinkers in philosophy, are essential elements of the cultural and intellectual renewal that you must foster in your country.

7. In closing this series of *Ad Limina* visits with the American bishops, I wish to express my warmest personal appreciation to you for the spiritual communion, solidarity, and support which you have shown me during the twenty years of my pontificate. I too feel that I am your friend and elder brother on the pilgrimage of faith and fidelity which together we are making in devotion to Christ and service of his Church. To the priests, religious, and laity of the United States, I express once more my cordial esteem and gratitude, asking the Holy Spirit to give your local churches a new outpouring of life and energy for the mission still to be fulfilled. I pray that there will be a continuing and all-embracing renewal of unity and love among all American Catholics, of reconciliation and mutual support in the truth of faith.

I ask God to bless your efforts in the ecumenical dialogue with other Christians and in interreligious cooperation on the basis of the many fundamental points of contact we share with all believers. My fervent prayer is that there will be a fresh spirit of goodness, harmony, and peace among all the people of the United States, so that your public life may be renewed in truthfulness and honor, and your country may carry out its historical destiny among the peoples of the world.

Commending you and your brother bishops to the loving care of Mary Immaculate, heavenly patron of the United States of America, I cordially impart my apostolic blessing.

FROM THE VATICAN, OCTOBER 24, 1998

Joannes Paulus II

APPENDIX:
LISTING OF BISHOPS
BY REGION

Region I

**States of Connecticut, Maine, Massachusetts,
New Hampshire, Rhode Island, and Vermont
Provinces of Boston and Hartford
Eparchy of Stamford and Eparchy for Melkites**

Bishop William F. Murphy,
    Chairman
Bishop Emilio Allué, SDB
Bishop Kenneth A. Angell
Bishop John P. Boles
Bishop Francis J. Christian
Bishop Michael R. Cote
Archbishop Daniel A. Cronin
Bishop Thomas L. Dupre
Bishop Edward M. Egan
Bishop John A. Elya, BSO
Bishop Louis E. Gelineau
Bishop Odore J. Gendron
Bishop Joseph J. Gerry, OSB
Bishop Daniel A. Hart
Bishop Francis X. Irwin

Cardinal Bernard Law
Bishop Basil H. Losten
Bishop Christie A. Macaluso
Bishop Joseph F. Maguire
Bishop John B. McCormack
Bishop John R. McNamara
Bishop Robert E. Mulvee
Bishop Edward C. O'Leary
Bishop Sean P. O'Malley,
    OFMCap
Bishop Daniel P. Reilly
Bishop Lawrence J. Riley
Bishop Peter A. Rosazza
Bishop George E. Rueger
Bishop Nicholas J. Samra
Bishop Joseph E. Tawil

Region II

State of New York
Province of New York
Eparchy of St. Maron and Apostolic Exarchate for Armenians

Bishop John R. McGann, Chairman

Bishop Patrick V. Ahern

Bishop Paulius A. Baltakis, OFM

Bishop Gerald M. Barbarito

Bishop Edwin B. Broderick

Bishop Robert A. Brucato

Bishop Ignatius A. Catanello

Bishop Matthew H. Clark

Bishop Thomas J. Costello

Bishop Thomas V. Daily

Bishop James J. Daly

Bishop Stephen Hector Doueihi

Bishop John C. Dunne

Bishop Francisco Garmendia

Bishop Edward M. Grosz

Bishop Frank J. Harrison

Bishop Edward D. Head

Bishop Dennis W. Hickey

Bishop Joseph L. Hogan

Bishop Howard J. Hubbard

Bishop Paul S. Loverde

Bishop James P. Mahoney

Bishop Henry J. Mansell

Archbishop Eugene A. Marino, SSJ

Bishop William J. McCormack

Bishop Bernard J. McLaughlin

Bishop Anthony F. Mestice

Bishop James M. Moynihan

Cardinal John O'Connor

Bishop Nerses M. Setian

Bishop Patrick J. Sheridan

Bishop Joseph M. Sullivan

Bishop Hovhannes Tertzakian, OMVen

Bishop René A. Valero

Bishop Austin B. Vaughan

Bishop Emil A. Wcela

Bishop Francis M. Zayek

Region III

States of New Jersey and Pennsylvania
Provinces of Newark and Philadelphia
Archeparchy of Philadelphia for Ukrainians, Archeparchy of
Pittsburgh for the Byzantine Ruthenians, Eparchy of Passaic, and
Our Lady of Deliverance of Newark of the Syrians

Bishop John M. Smith, Chairman

Bishop Joseph V. Adamec

Bishop David Arias, OAR

Cardinal Anthony Bevilacqua

Bishop Paul G. Bootkoski

Bishop Anthony G. Bosco

Bishop Vincent D. Breen

Bishop Edward P. Cullen

Bishop Nicholas C. Dattilo

Bishop Louis A. DeSimone

Bishop Nicholas A. DiMarzio

Bishop John M. Dougherty

Bishop Michael J. Dudick

Bishop Robert F. Garner

Archbishop Peter L. Gerety

Bishop John J. Graham

Bishop James J. Hogan

Bishop Edward T. Hughes

Bishop Martin N. Lohmuller

Bishop Robert P. Maginnis

Bishop Dominic A. Marconi

Bishop Joseph F. Martino

Archbishop Theodore E. McCarrick

Bishop Charles J. McDonnell

Bishop John B. McDowell

Bishop James T. McHugh

Bishop Michael J. Murphy

Bishop Walter Paska

Bishop Andrew Pataki

Archbishop Judson M. Procyk

Bishop John C. Reiss

Bishop Frank J. Rodimer

Bishop James L. Schad

Archbishop Stephen M. Sulyk

Bishop James C. Timlin

Bishop Donald W. Trautman

Bishop Thomas J. Welsh

Bishop William J. Winter

Bishop Donald W. Wuerl

Bishop Joseph Younan

Bishop David A. Zubik

Region IV

States of Delaware, District of Columbia, Florida, Georgia, Maryland, North Carolina, South Carolina, Virginia, West Virginia, and the Territory of the Virgin Islands Provinces of Atlanta, Baltimore, Miami, Washington, and the Ordinariate for Military Services USA

Bishop Michael A. Saltarelli, Chairman
Bishop Michael J. Begley
Bishop Gordon D. Bennett, SJ
Bishop J. Kevin Boland
Archbishop William D. Borders
Bishop Walter A. Coggin, OSB
Bishop Alvaro Corrada del Rio, SJ
Bishop William G. Curlin
Archbishop Joseph T. Dimino
Archbishop John F. Donoghue
Bishop Norbert M. Dorsey, CP
Archbishop John C. Favalora
Bishop Gilberto Fernandez
Bishop John J. Glynn
Bishop F. Joseph Gossman
Bishop Thomas J. Grady
Cardinal James Hickey
Bishop John R. Keating
Cardinal William Keeler
Bishop W. Thomas Larkin
Bishop Raymond W. Lessard
Bishop William E. Lori

Bishop George E. Lynch
Bishop Robert N. Lynch
Bishop Joseph J. Madera, MSpS
Bishop Edmund F. McCaffrey, OSB
Archbishop Edward A. McCarthy
Bishop James E. Michaels, SSCME
Bishop P. Francis Murphy
Bishop John J. Nevins
Bishop William C. Newman
Archbishop Edwin F. O'Brien
Bishop Leonard J. Olivier, SVD
Bishop John H. Ricard, SSJ
Bishop Agustín A. Román
Bishop Francis X. Roque
Archbishop Joseph T. Ryan
Bishop Bernard W. Schmitt
Bishop John J. Snyder
Bishop Walter F. Sullivan
Bishop J. Keith Symons
Bishop Elliott G. Thomas
Bishop David B. Thompson
Bishop Thomas G. Wenski

Region V

States of Alabama, Kentucky, Louisiana, Mississippi, and Tennessee
Provinces of Louisville, Mobile, and New Orleans

Bishop Edward U. Kmiec,
Chairman
Bishop Gregory M. Aymond
Bishop Dominic Carmon, SVD
Bishop David E. Foley
Bishop Gerard L. Frey
Bishop William B. Friend
Archbishop Philip M. Hannan
Bishop William R. Houck
Bishop Joseph L. Howze
Bishop Alfred C. Hughes
Bishop William A. Hughes
Bishop Sam G. Jacobs
Bishop Michael Jarrell

Archbishop Thomas C. Kelly, OP
Archbishop Oscar H. Lipscomb
Bishop Charles G. Maloney
Archbishop Thomas J.
McDonough
Bishop John J. McRaith
Bishop Robert W. Muench
Bishop James D. Niedergeses
Bishop Anthony J. O'Connell
Bishop Edward J. O'Donnell
Archbishop Francis B. Schulte
Bishop Jude Speyrer
Bishop J. Terry Steib, SVD
Bishop J. Kendrick Williams

Region VI

States of Michigan and Ohio
Provinces of Cincinnati and Detroit
Eparchy of Parma, Apostolic Exarchate for Chaldeans, and
Apostolic Exarchate for Romanians

Bishop Thomas J. Tobin,
Chairman
Bishop Moses B. Anderson, SSE
Bishop John Michael Botean
Bishop Joseph M. Breitenbeck
Bishop Kevin M. Britt
Bishop Patrick R. Cooney
Bishop Robert W. Donnelly
Bishop Paul V. Donovan
Bishop Benedict C. Franzetta
Bishop James H. Garland
Bishop James A. Griffin
Bishop Thomas J. Gumbleton
Bishop Bernard J. Harrington
Bishop Edward J. Herrmann
Bishop James R. Hoffman
Bishop Ibrahim N. Ibrahim
Bishop Arthur H. Krawczak
Cardinal Adam Maida
Bishop James W. Malone

Bishop Joseph C. McKinney
Bishop Carl F. Mengeling
Bishop Carl K. Moeddel
Bishop Robert M. Moskal
Bishop James A. Murray
Bishop John C. Nienstedt
Bishop Albert H. Ottenweller
Bishop A. Edward Pevec
Archbishop Daniel E. Pilarczyk
Bishop Anthony M. Pilla
Bishop Kenneth J. Povish
Bishop Louis Puscas
Bishop A. James Quinn
Bishop Robert J. Rose
Bishop Mark F. Schmitt
Bishop Walter J. Schoenherr
Bishop Basil Schott, OFM
Bishop Gilbert I. Sheldon
Bishop Kenneth E. Untener
Bishop Allen H. Vigneron

Region VII

States of Illinois, Indiana, and Wisconsin
Provinces of Chicago, Indianapolis, and Milwaukee
Eparchy of St. Nicholas in Chicago–Ukrainian

Bishop Thomas G. Doran,
    Chairman
Bishop Alfred L. Abramowicz
Bishop Robert J. Banks
Archbishop Daniel M. Buechlein,
    OSB
Bishop William H. Bullock
Bishop Raymond L. Burke
Bishop Edwin M. Conway
Bishop Joseph R. Crowley
Bishop John M. D'Arcy
Bishop Raphael M. Fliss
Bishop Frederick W. Freking
Bishop Norbert F. Gaughan
Cardinal Francis George, OMI
Bishop Gerald A. Gettelfinger
Bishop Raymond E. Goedert
Bishop John R. Gorman
Bishop Wilton D. Gregory
Bishop William L. Higi
Bishop Joseph L. Imesch
Bishop Thad J. Jakubowski
Bishop Daniel R. Jenky, CSC

Bishop Roger L. Kaffer
Bishop Gerald F. Kicanas
Bishop Innocent H. Lotocky,
    OSBM
Bishop Timothy J. Lyne
Bishop John R. Manz
Bishop Dale J. Melczek
Bishop Robert F. Morneau
Bishop George V. Murry, SJ
Bishop John J. Myers
Bishop Arthur J. O'Neill
Bishop Edward W. O'Rourke
Bishop John J. Paul
Bishop Leo A. Pursley
Bishop Daniel L. Ryan
Bishop John R. Sheets, SJ
Bishop Richard J. Sklba
Archbishop Rembert G.
    Weakland, OSB
Bishop George O. Wirz
Bishop Michael Wiwchar, CSSR
Bishop Aloysius J. Wycislo

Region VIII

States of Minnesota, North Dakota, and South Dakota
Province of St. Paul and Minneapolis

Bishop Lawrence H. Welsh,
Chairman
Bishop Victor Balke
Bishop Robert J. Carlson
Bishop Paul V. Dudley
Archbishop Harry J. Flynn
Bishop J. Richard Ham
Bishop John F. Kinney

Bishop Raymond A. Lucker
Archbishop John R. Roach
Bishop Roger L. Schwietz, OMI
Bishop George H. Speltz
Bishop James S. Sullivan
Bishop Loras J. Watters
Bishop Paul A. Zipfel

Region IX

**States of Iowa, Kansas, Missouri, and Nebraska
Provinces of Dubuque, Kansas City in Kansas,
Omaha, and St. Louis**

Bishop Daniel N. DiNardo,
Chairman
Bishop Raymond J. Boland
Bishop Edward K. Braxton
Bishop Fabian W. Bruskewitz
Cardinal John Carberry
Bishop Joseph L. Charron, CPPS
Archbishop Elden F. Curtiss
Bishop George K. Fitzsimons
Bishop Marion F. Forst
Bishop William E. Franklin
Bishop John R. Gaydos
Bishop Eugene J. Gerber
Bishop George J. Gottwald
Archbishop Jerome G. Hanus,
OSB

Archbishop James P. Keleher
Archbishop Daniel W. Kucera,
OSB
Bishop John J. Leibrecht
Bishop Michael F. McAuliffe
Bishop Lawrence J. McNamara
Bishop Joseph Naumann
Bishop Gerald F. O'Keefe
Bishop John L. Paschang
Archbishop Justin F. Rigali
Bishop Stanley G. Schlarman
Archbishop Daniel E. Sheehan
Bishop Michael J. Sheridan
Bishop Lawrence D. Soens
Archbishop Ignatius J. Strecker
Bishop John J. Sullivan

Region X

States of Arkansas, Oklahoma, and Texas—excluding El Paso
Provinces of Oklahoma City and San Antonio

Bishop Edward J. Slattery,
Chairman

Archbishop Eusebius J. Beltran

Bishop Edmond Carmody

Bishop Joseph P. Delaney

Bishop David E. Fellhauer

Bishop Joseph A. Fiorenza

Bishop John J. Fitzpatrick

Bishop Thomas J. Flanagan

Archbishop Patrick F. Flores

Bishop Joseph A. Galante

Bishop Roberto O. González,
OFM

Bishop Rene H. Gracida

Bishop Charles V. Grahmann

Bishop Curtis J. Guillory, SVD

Bishop Leroy T. Matthiesen

Bishop John E. McCarthy

Bishop Andrew J. McDonald

Bishop Raymundo J. Peña

Bishop Michael D. Pfeifer, OMI

Bishop Bernard F. Popp

Bishop Placido Rodríguez, CMF

Archbishop Charles A. Salatka

Bishop James A. Tamayo

Bishop Thomas A. Tschoepe

Bishop John W. Yanta

Bishop Patrick J. Zurek

Region XI

States of California, Hawaii, and Nevada
Provinces of Los Angeles and
San Francisco—excluding Salt Lake City
Eparchy of Van Nuys

Bishop Daniel F. Walsh,
Chairman
Bishop Juan A. Arzube
Bishop Gerald R. Barnes
Bishop Stephen E. Blaire
Bishop Robert H. Brom
Bishop Gilbert E. Chávez
Bishop John G. Chedid
Bishop Harry A. Clinch
Bishop John S. Cummins
Bishop Thomas J. Curry
Bishop Francis X. DiLorenzo
Bishop Michael P. Driscoll
Bishop R. Pierre DuMaine
Bishop Joseph A. Ferrario
Bishop Richard J. Garcia
Bishop Mark J. Hurley

Archbishop William J. Levada
Cardinal Roger Mahony
Bishop Norman F. McFarland
Bishop Patrick J. McGrath
Bishop Donald W. Montrose
Bishop Francis A. Quinn
Archbishop John R. Quinn
Bishop Sylvester D. Ryan
Bishop Joseph M. Sartoris
Bishop John T. Steinbock
Bishop Phillip F. Straling
Bishop John J. Ward
Bishop William K. Weigand
Bishop Gerald E. Wilkerson
Bishop Gabino Zavala
Bishop G. Patrick Ziemann

Region XII

States of Alaska, Idaho, Montana, Oregon, and Washington
Provinces of Anchorage, Portland, and Seattle

Archbishop Francis T. Hurley, Chairman

Bishop Tod D. Brown

Archbishop Alexander J. Brunett

Bishop Thomas J. Connolly

Archbishop Raymond G. Hunthausen

Bishop Michael J. Kaniecki, SJ

Bishop Anthony M. Milone

Bishop Eldon B. Schuster

Bishop Carlos A. Sevilla, SJ

Bishop William S. Skylstad

Bishop Kenneth Steiner

Archbishop John G. Vlazny

Bishop Michael Warfel

Bishop Robert L. Whelan, SJ

Region XIII

**States of Utah, Arizona, New Mexico, Colorado, and Wyoming
Provinces of Denver, Santa Fe, part of San Francisco
(Salt Lake City), and part of Texas (El Paso)**

Bishop Manuel D. Moreno,
Chairman
Bishop Charles A. Buswell
Archbishop Charles J. Chaput,
OFMCap
Bishop J. Lennox Federal
Bishop Richard C. Hanifen
Bishop Joseph H. Hart
Bishop George M. Kuzma

Bishop George H. Niederauer
Bishop Thomas J. O'Brien
Bishop Armando X. Ochoa
Bishop Donald E. Pelotte, SSS
Bishop Ricardo Ramírez, CSB
Archbishop Robert F. Sanchez
Archbishop Michael J. Sheehan
Bishop Arthur N. Tafoya

SUBJECT INDEX